THE
INVISIBLE
NATURE OF YAHWEH

Dr. Tracey L. Milan

THE INVISIBLE NATURE OF YAHWEH

by Dr. Tracey L. Milan

Published by One Faith Publishing
Richmond, VA
onefaithpublishings@gmail.com

This book or parts thereof may not be reproduced in any form, stored in a retrieval system, or transmitted in any forms by any means -electronic, mechanical, photocopy, recording, or otherwise-written without written permission of the publisher and/or author, Dr. Tracey L. Milan, except as provided by United States of America copyright law.

Unless otherwise noted, all Scripture quotations marked (NIV) are from the Holy Bible, New International Version. Copyright © 1973, 1978, 1984. 2011 by Biblica, Used by permission of Zondervan and public domain. All rights reserved worldwide.

THE HOLY BIBLE, NEW INTERNATIONAL VERSION®, NIV® Copyright © 1973, 1978, 1984, 2011 by Biblica, Inc.™ Used by permission. All rights reserved worldwide.

The Holy Bible, English Standard Version® (ESV®) Copyright © 2001 by Crossway, a publishing ministry of Good News Publishers. All rights reserved.

Scriptures marked RSV are taken from the REVISED STANDARD VERSION (RSV): Scripture taken from the REVISED STANDARD VERSION, Grand Rapids: Zondervan, 1971.

Scriptures marked MKJV are taken from the MODERN KING JAMES VERSION (MKJV): Scripture taken from the Holy Bible, MODERN KING JAMES VERSION copyright© 1962 – 1998 by Jay P. Green, Sr. Used by permission of the copyright holder.

Scriptures marked TLB are taken from the THE LIVING BIBLE (TLB): Scripture taken from THE LIVING BIBLE copyright© 1971. Used by permission of Tyndale House Publishers, Inc., Carol Stream, Illinois 60188. All rights reserved.

Scriptures marked NKJV are taken from the NEW KING JAMES VERSION (NKJV): Scripture taken from the NEW KING JAMES VERSION®. Copyright© 1982 by Thomas Nelson, Inc. Used by permission. All rights reserved.

The Hebrew lexicon is Brown, Driver, Briggs, Gesenius Lexicon; this is keyed to the "Theological Word Book of the Old Testament." These files are considered public domain.

The Living Bible copyright © 1971 by Tyndale House Foundation. Used by permission of Tyndale House Publishers Inc., Carol Stream, Illinois 60188. All rights reserved. The Living Bible, TLB, and the The Living Bible logo are registered trademarks of Tyndale House Publishers

Holy Bible, New Living Translation, copyright © 1996, 2004, 2007, 2013, 2015 by Tyndale House Foundation. Used by permission of Tyndale House Publishers Inc., Carol Stream, Illinois 60188. All rights reserved.

Copyright © 2019 by Dr. Tracey L. Milan.
All rights reserved.

TABLE OF CONTENTS

Acknowledgments 4

Preface 5

Chapter 1 Reason 15

Chapter 2 Does God choose to remain Invisible? 32

Chapter 3 The Spiritual Incarnation of Yahweh 53

Chapter 4 The Invisibility in Jesus Christ (Yeshua HaMaschiach) 59

Chapter 5 Confidence Of Light 77

Chapter 6 The Invisibility Of God Before Us 88

Chapter 7 Sanctification by Authority 112

Chapter 8 Looking Beyond 119

Chapter 9 The Gift Of The Light (Light Treasures) 133

Chapter 10 Divine Ranks 147

Chapter 11 Yahweh Directs The Human Spirit 166

Chapter 12 Yahweh's Visibility as Truth 189

References 201

About The Author 204

A word from Dr. Milan 205

ACKNOWLEDGMENTS

I would like to acknowledge the indwelling Spirit that has directed me to this place in my life, for wisdom, protection, favor, and security. "Yahweh, The Invisible Spirit" joined by "The Word in the Holy Spirit that has brought Elohim in the form of Wisdom to this place of understanding."

To my wife and my daughter, who both supported me spiritually through my struggles. They stayed the course. Thank you!

To my parents, who both recognized my calling into the realm of understanding. To my brothers Ira L. Milan, who listened and challenged my thoughts in this realm of my growth and development, and to Alvert "Big Al" Milan for staying the course with me.

To the Publisher Tammy Swafford and all the other authors' source materials that supported my writings, I am truly thankful!

To the Invisible Spirit of the "Most High," there is no shift in its conviction to the created creature called the human. In harmony, we ask, and the door is open!

PREFACE

A question comes to mind...

Has God changed anytime throughout time?

Has Jesus or the Holy Spirit ever changed?

The creatures that God created evolved, which means change; nonetheless, God wasn't evolving, The Word wasn't changing, nor was the Holy Spirit, but based on religion, change was inevitable. Our spiritual tables set before us dictated the change, meaning, this draws us to the place, as long as we are part of a social setting, where we will continually move forward evolving as humans in religion, theology, mental and physical health, politics, human rights, race, social awareness, technology, etc. These changes must take place for us to perfect our spiritual standards, which are set in place for our reconciliation with God. Therefore, we are not changing; we're only perfecting our standards in truth and righteousness based on whom and whose we truly are, and we are the undeniable remnant of the *"Most High."*

Early in the picture, we were lifeless in our understanding of scripture. We were dead in our transgressions and wandered as if we were in the forty-year desert experience and in need of directions to God's promise. It appears as though we have a similar vortex in modern times; religion has brought us to this paradigm, and once again, we don't know which way to go. We're in the midst of confusion based on a melting pot of theologies, denominationalism, and scenarios about how to win God's favor in a mirage of belief systems, with each having its own captive value system to lure us in.

God will never change,

"God is not human, that He should lie, not a human being, that He should change His mind. Does He speak and then not act? Does He promise and not fulfill?"
-Numbers 23:19

The Word will endure to the end of times. The Holy Spirit will continue to exist within our midst. We will continue to transcend time in these bodies; we, the creature, will continue to evolve, but towards what? When we examine what the scripture states about our continual evolution, *"We were created in the image of God"* that should direct us someplace, a place that is connected to God, which is the Son Jesus, who has left us, not alone, but with a comforter in the Holy Spirit, which Yeshua described as the giver of truth and righteousness.

"Peter said to them, "Each one of you must turn away from your sins and be baptized in the name of Jesus Christ, so that your sins will be forgiven, and you will receive God's gift, the Holy Spirit." -Acts 2:38

The Holy Spirit is invisible, but what about YAHWEH? Yes, this Spirit is also invisible, and Yeshua, who was made visible in the flesh, except with an invisible spirit of Yahweh that resembles our flesh and spirit in every way.

The Invisible Nature Of Yahweh

"For since the creation of the world God's invisible qualities-this eternal power and divine nature-have been clearly seen, being understood from what has been made, so that people are without excuse" -Romans 1:20

Without any doubt, the world that we live in is in chaos, just as it was when men first justified the world as barbaric or until now a modern civilization; as in the beginning, the world was chaos in an unformed mass. To preclude, one must look at Yahweh's invisible nature and understand why man, God's creation, with a humus body, which internalizes an invisible spirit, has not recognized the invisibility of God within them. The human is the key; we are the authority that can break the hold of barbarism and chaos, but we must first realize that he/she is a mystery to one another and that God is a non-material personal being self-conscious and self-determining. On the other hand, we as humans must master the connection between man's domination in the psychological sense and compel our interest in the spiritual nature of the unseen.

In contemplation, this book is a compilation of ruminations that pull together the thoughts of the creative energy that poses the intellect of those who have placed interest in the thought of the invisible nature of Yahweh. All too often, we find ourselves subjective to who we are; where is our "Creator," and why does He hide from us? God has glorified creation and desires that we look past our thoughts and ways and focus on the truths He has placed before us. In a writing by Robert E. Kofahl, he states his research towards God as being involved in His creation and someone whom we should know better:

> *"God is someone we can get to know. He, unlike ourselves, doesn't need to be told what to do. On the other hand, He tells us what to do and how to live in a manner pleasing to Him. Just because He can't be seen by the human eye doesn't mean He is not there and, therefore, should be ignored. Quite the opposite is true; His creation demonstrates His existence. Also, since he cannot be seen, we need to devote ourselves to study everything that has been written about Him (Yahweh) so that we can know Him like He wants us to and begin to live our lives in a way that pleases Him."* Robert E. Kofahl

God is other than what we, as humans, consider Him to be. We only fool ourselves into revelations about Him based on what we read and the historical fascinations that have been scribbled by the pen that is handled by the deceptive creature that denies the integrity God has placed in us,

"How can we say, "We are wise, for we have the law of the Lord," when actually the lying pen of the scribes has handled it falsely."
-Jeremiah. 8:8

"God is a spirit: and they that worship him must worship in spirit and in truth."
-John 4:24

Can we truly facilitate our pragmatic mindset in a non-realistic contrast, knowing we're inside a syndrome based on theoretical dichotomy, which is based on what is held as fascist mysticism and mistruths? Our clannish existence has driven us into exile just as our biblical history has proven.

Without understanding the true image of God, we are recreating the broken beliefs of our ancestors. They gave up on Yahweh due to the fact that God could act upon their emotions and prove to them that He was in their midst. Yahweh knew them better than they knew themselves, but this was hindsight to them; our ancestors wanted the tangible example placed before them just as we do today. Humans want God just as they see the little gods that bring them pleasure each day.

> *"God has no image, He cannot be seen by the human eye, but creation points to His existence. His Son, Jesus, testified to this existence and desire to be sought by His*

creatures. He also provided us with an example of how to live our lives seeking and serving God."

In this understanding about Yahweh, we are not in awe of his invisibility, because we aren't aware of who and what we are. God placed Him in the flesh as the salvation to creation, but we are aware of our worldview of survival only in this syndrome that we call life! We amass idols to fulfill the reason we are here in our humus bodies; this reasoning only brings about in the form of deception that cancels out the true relationship of invisibility of God in us. There are many reasons we're here on earth, but the primary reason is so our feelings about Yahweh won't disappear while in this flesh. The unseen nature of Yahweh longs to love us and has an eternal experience with us for eternity. Our earthly experience poses the first trial that we must pass while in these dirt-encrusted bodies.

Throughout our lives, we have been taught in error the survival skills that serve the elitist, their cultures, and their traditions. Cages have been placed before us. We go in and out of these cages during our lifetime, but we must realize we have the power to open and close the door to our cages, and most importantly, we are the proverbial lock and key, so before you confine yourself to a cage, know first that you have the authority to lock and unlock your confinement. This key that consists of your internal wisdom given by Yahweh will unlock the power of the Kingdom and make it work in our lives.

Knowledge leads to understanding, and once we comprehend the principles behind the keys, we can understand how they work in the Kingdom here on earth. This is exactly the problem with many believers today. We have "keys" that mimic "Scriptures" that most of us don't know how to use. We have an abundance of keys, but we don't know which key unlocks which lock pertaining to any particular scripture. It's like having all this information from the bible but not knowing how to unlock its meanings. We have all this power available to us but do not know how to apply it. This is how we become prisoners in cages. We're in and out of cages in repetitive cycles due to a lack of knowledge.

Knowledge is power, and we must get our power back! The Word of God is important but insufficient by itself for effective living as a believer. This is because most believers lack a proper Kingdom mindset. Life in the Kingdom is really about returning to the true laws that are the governing authority of God in the earth and learning how to live and function in that authority. We are the authority, so knowing why and how you were placed in the visible Kingdom here on earth gives us the right to partake as Kingdom citizens.

Part of understanding the Kingdom is learning how to use the keys (authority) of the Kingdom. The Kingdom of Heaven is God's desire and purpose for us. Yahweh's desire for us is to experience HIS true revelation for His creation on earth. God doesn't need us in heaven. HE brought heaven to the visible earth for us to witness HIS Kingdom to come, on earth as it is in Heaven! The Kingdom of heaven is not placed out of sight. It's the visible Kingdom that was placed on this planet. Yahweh placed the invisible Kingdom on a visible planet called earth; God colonized earth with the inherent qualities of heaven, but we must learn how to unlock its laws that have been bound by Satan and his *ecclesia*. These keys have to be taught and learned.

A secret is anything that hasn't been shared, especially if somebody else is hiding the information. Supernatural occurrences fall into this category, sometimes referred to as a miracle. This is something that humans cannot explain. It's an event or occurrence that
seems to defy the laws of nature. "These men had seen Jesus walk on water, heal the sick, raise the dead, shrivel a tree by speaking to it, calm a storm, multiply bread, and many other "miraculous" things that were beyond the ken of human experience. But to Jesus, none of those were miracles. He said, "These are no miracles; I'm just using keys. I know how to put them in the locks, and they are unlocking prosperity, unlocking healing, unlocking peace, unlocking authority. Watch, you and I will see the Kingdom at work, and also how it should work for us. My Father has given you the knowledge of the secrets of the Kingdom. I will teach you how to use the keys." Jesus left no doubt that the Kingdom was supposed to work for His *ecclesia* just as it worked for Him, for the night before His death He told them:

"I tell you the truth; anyone who has faith in Me will do what I have been doing. He will do even greater things than these, because I am going to the Father. And I will do whatever you ask in My name, so that the Son may bring

glory to the Father. You may ask Me for anything in My name, and I will do it."
 -John 14:12-14

Chapter 1

Reason

For the masses, confusion is the fuel that drives us to our final destination, which is called eternal life or for another place termed as hell. These two terms can be defined as realities or metaphors; we live them both but haven't experienced them inside our creator; there is no confusion in the truth.

Confusion is a state of mind that blocks us from the relevancy of the invisible nature that exists within us, this connection in the invisible realm outside our state of mind, which is coined as our divinity, which is a divine state of existence. Outside of divinity, confusion exists, which fuels fear, which brings doubt, and in return, brings about ruin.

"For God did not give us a spirit of fear, but of power and love and of a sound mind.
So do not be ashamed of the testimony about our Lord or of me his prisoner."

-2 Timothy 1:7-8

We are all Yahweh's prisoners, not in the sense of being behind metal bars, but in a flesh type captivity. Our testimonies are based on our survival skills while in these humus bodies; we have all been given the gift of the spirit, but as we are confined to these bodies, God gives us a way out in the form of spirit, an invisible quality that reflects His image, character, and integrity.

While in these bodies, our designation is truth, righteousness, love, and holiness. The purpose is based on a special status that is officially bestowed from above this realm. God is love; The Spirit desires that we be captive in its bindless love, but we are prisoners of the false gods of wood, metal, and stone *(Deuteronomy 4:28, Isaiah 44)*, which are forms of idolatry that turn our flesh towards the spirits of the metaphorical Satan, which are power, money, and the weakened flesh. We must turn away from the false deity of fear and seek the invisible God that dwells amongst us *(The Holy Spirit)* and inside of us *(The Eternal Spirit)*, both instituted by Yahweh.

This is the "Kingdom" that must come. Paul Finney, in his book *"The Invisible God,"* explains this concept,

> *"On the idea of seeing divinity and representing visually what is seen, early Christianity was shaped by three ancient concepts: first, that humans could have a direct vision of God; second, that they could not; and, third, that*

although humans could see God, they were best advised not to look and were strictly forbidden to represent what they had seen. The first of these three, the iconic view of divinity, came to early Christians over long routes from early Indo-European religions in the Aegean and from their Semitic counterparts in the ancient Near East. The classic Western expression is found in the seventh and eighth centuries, within the circle of Homeric/Hesiodic mythopoesis, a tradition that was very much alive in both the Greco-Roman and the Greco-Semitic worlds that played host to the earliest Christians."

"In large part, the earliest Christians rejected the iconic view of divinity. The idea that humans could see divinity appearing in either anthropomorphic or theriomorphic (for example, the Cretan Zeus: a bull) guise is a concept the early Christians (especially the apologists) found absurd. Christian writers ridiculed the people who upheld this notion, and likewise, they impugned the idea itself, often in elaborately constructed rhetorical conceits. The second-and third-century apologist treated the iconic view of divinity as a literary foil, which gave them leave to

propound a different-and-they thought better-concept of divinity. Most of the new religionists' rejection of this iconic view appears within the pages of early Christian apology."

"The second of these three ancient concepts, that humans cannot see God because God is invisible, also has a long pedigree, though slightly shorter than the first. In the West, this concept is linked to philosophy, and the earliest identifiable traces are located in the east Aegean during the sixth century B.C., among the pre-Socratics, notably Xenophanes. This concept involves the definition of an abstract divinity that is unlike anything or anybody we encounter in the world of daily experience. Indeed it is precisely the imperfections of this world, its contingents, and transitory nature, together with our habit of relying on sensorial experience to interpret life in this world, which provides the building blocks for the construction of a negative theological paradigm that defines the God of philosophy. This is a God of apophasis predicates, a divinity who, for example, cannot be known or contained or represented or defined or seen."

We cannot see God because we cannot see the examples He has placed before us; the first is seeing ourselves as a "Spiritual" creation instead of seeing one another as just fleshly objects. Judging the outer influence is the current standard set forth by humans. This in part, stagnates our flesh to conform to its surroundings and wage spiritual warfare in reference to what we like and dislike.

We transcend through time, not recognizing that we have the ability to transcend. This within itself relates to the Holy Spirit, as it resembles our true spirit transcending without a fleshly body. The Spirit carries itself throughout time and space. The only thing that keeps our spirit grounded on earth in a divine state is our fleshly bodies. It's not so much the material appearance of what we look like or based on what we see while we're in these fleshly bodies, but it is what we are designed to do while we are in them, and that's why it is so important to recognize and relate to our concealed spirit *(We don't have a spirit; we are a spirit),*

"However, you are not in the flesh but in the Spirit, if indeed the Spirit of God dwells in you. But if anyone does not have the Spirit of Christ, he does not belong to Him"
-Romans 8:9

In locution, we must make an effort to understand our eternal spirit fully, *"The Invisible Nature of Yahweh"* that resides in and amongst us. Our internal spirit desires the equivalence of the Holy Spirit. It sees what the flesh denies;

this denial of sight is a form of suppression that seems to have been present since Adam's fall.

Thus, when Cicero's expositor of Stoic theology, Balbus, declares that *"Nothing is more difficult than to divert the mind from the habit of reliance on the eyes,"* this is a statement designed to wean humans, educated and uneducated alike, from the erroneous habit of theological anthropomorphism- that is, imagining divinity in human form.

Xenophon's Socrates (Mem. 4.3.13ff.), Tat in the Hermetic corpus (Logos 5.1-6), Jesus instructing Philip (Jn 14:8-11ff), and Theophilus (Autol. II.1ff)

Writings to Autolycus all share the same message: God is invisible, and it is an exercise in futility for humans either to imagine God in human form or to seek an unmediated vision of the divine eidos.

We will see God when we train our eyes to see the true nature of the divinity of His creation, godliness, holiness, and the Godhead, who is Yahshua the divinity of EL ELYON. Our purpose in this life is to inhabit the Spirit and to understand the vibrations that were once set before us (the hearing) and have now been manipulated from entering into the true temple of God (the humus body). This temple is the holy residing and resting place of the Holy Spirit. This temple desires to hear the Holy resonance vibrations from God. When we were less, we were mightier than we are now spiritually, in that too many negative frequencies are forced upon the temple of the humus creature to hear the truth of God, His triune nature. In this, we can't sense God's invisibility; therefore, we can't see ourselves in the spiritual sense.

The kingdom of man has filled us with their mentalities; in other words, we are filled with their religions and belief systems of **S**uppressive, **H**armful, **I**ntrusive, **T**houghts! Yahweh is invisible. The man that El created isn't invisible, which leaves the created creature exposed, and this alone should bring us to a place of understanding that we need coverage in this realm to deflect what has been placed against the invisible spirit inside our fleshly bodies. Robert Deffinbaugh defends and expands this thought by saying:

"And while He will be invisible to the world after His ascension, He will be very evident to those who believe in Him. They will sense His presence more surely, and He will no longer dwell among them but in them. The "invisible" presence of our Lord is better than His visible presence was. We are privileged to know God more intimately now after our Lord's death, resurrection, and ascension than men ever knew Him before".

"Here we can clearly discern God eternal, incarnate in the Son as invisible to the world after the ascension; it will take discernment from believers to understand the transparency of God's invisibility by way of the incarnated flesh that housed this hidden spirit that was

concealed, and indiscernible by those who didn't have faith."

Robert Deffinbaugh gives his view concerning the invisibility of God in this way:

"Some may believe the Bible is self-contradicting regarding God's invisibility. Some texts clearly indicate that God is invisible, that He cannot be seen:

"No man has seen God at any time; the only begotten God, who is in the bosom of the Father, He has explained Him" -John 1:18

"Now to the King eternal, immortal, invisible, the only God, be honor and glory forever and ever. Amen" -1 Timothy 1:17

But there are also texts where men claim to have seen God:

"So Jacob named the place Peniel, for he said, "I have seen God face to face, yet my life has been preserved" -Genesis 32:30.

"Thus the Lord used to speak to Moses face to face, just as a man speaks to his friend. When Moses returned to the

camp, his servant Joshua, the son of Nun, a young man, would not depart from the tent" -Exodus 33:11

"And they will tell it to the inhabitants of this land. They have heard that Thou, O Lord, art in the midst of this people, for Thou, O Lord, art seen eye to eye, while Thy cloud stands over them; and Thou dost go before them in a pillar of cloud by day and a pillar of fire by night." - Numbers 14:14 (KJV)

"In light of the statements of some texts that God is invisible and others that men have seen God, let us lay down applicable biblical truths to help us resolve these apparent contradictions."

"Then the Lord spoke to you from the midst of the fire; you heard the sound of words, but you saw no form—only a voice" -Deuteronomy 4:12

"And the Father who sent Me, He has borne witness of Me. You have neither heard His voice at any time, nor seen His form" -John 5:37

Both the Old Testament and the New indicate to us that God has no form; that is, God has no physical body. Our efforts in defining Yahweh's physical presence only become futile. Great artists have depicted paintings or sculptures that depict the physical presence of Jesus Christ, but none have eluded to painting or creating a statue of Yahweh. Maybe the reason is that our internal spirit knows the truth; that nobody has ever seen Him but has seen the Son. The statements made about the "art" as being the presence of Yahweh, the examples of infused matter that takes form as nature and atmosphere, can be considered as God before us. The reason for this is explained by our Lord in His Words to the woman at the well:

"God is spirit, and those who worship Him must worship in spirit and truth" -John 4:24

Our faith is the component that drives us to a more complete sound doctrine of the visible.

This woman made reference to the dispute between the Jews and the Samaritans about the place where God was to be worshipped. The Jews were to worship God at Jerusalem, and Jesus could have corrected her by pointing this out, but He did not do so. Jesus informed her that, because of His incarnation, worship would never be the same. Specifically, worship would no longer be restricted to any one place. Men were to have worshipped God in Jerusalem because that is where God chose for His presence to dwell.

However, when God took on humanity at the incarnation (the coming of Christ to the earth), God chose to dwell not only *among* His people but also *in* His people. When Jesus ascended into heaven, the Holy Spirit came to indwell the church (The humus temple). The church can worship God anywhere because God's presence among men is spiritual, not physical. God is spirit, which means He is not restricted to one place, nor is worship any longer restricted to one place. God is invisible because He is spirit, not flesh.

Here, Bob Deffinbaugh puts together a great depiction of God's invisible nature by what is not seen but what is written in scripture that shapes the image of the invisibility of God to be where His creation believes He will be, and that is, God cannot be restricted to one place because He indwells all things, persons, places, all creation, and His will to be invisible beyond any anthropomorphisms spoken. His obscured nature is to be regarded and equated as faith as the *substance of things not seen and the evidence of things to come.* Bob Deffinbaugh imposes another thought, *"Should the Christian throw up his hands in despair? Is the Bible full of errors and inconsistencies, as some skeptics have alleged?"*

The Bible is the Christian's source for literacy as it relates to the visibility of God as the Christ, but there seems to be a lack of prudent information for us to be truly engaged in this matter of the invisibility of God. *"When does God appear to men, the descriptions of His appearance are sometimes vague?"* Here Deffinbaugh makes an analogy concerning Jacob's interaction with a "man" that he wrestled with. The vagueness is in what we've come to expect as to who this man is. Was it God or an angel of God? Who is any man to grapple with The GOD Most High? Here, we can discern the anthropomorphisms presented in the text:

"Then Jacob was left alone, and a man wrestled with him until daybreak.

And when he saw that he had not prevailed against him, he touched the socket of his thigh, so the socket of Jacob's thigh was dislocated while he wrestled with him.

Then he said, "Let me go, for the dawn is breaking." But he said, "I will not let you go unless you bless me."

So he said to him, "What is your name?" And he said, "Jacob."

And he said, "Your name shall no longer be Jacob, but Israel; for you have striven with God and with men and have prevailed."

Then Jacob asked him and said, "Please tell me your name." But he said, "Why is it that you ask my name?" And he blessed him there.

So Jacob named the place Peniel, for he said, "I have seen God face to face, yet my life has been preserved" -Genesis 32:24-30

Would God pity Himself to a mere human, especially Jacob? But the question that comes to mind is, would God give a human creature the time to ask what his name is? Is God not wise? Should God be made advisable by man? There isn't any relevance to God's invisible nature here in these passages, but more so of God's ability to utilize that which He chooses to awaken in man in his humus existence to receive instructions through the transcendence of the Holy Spirit. The Holy Spirit was advancing man as it traveled towards reconciliation with its glorified creation. The presence of God's Spirit was upon Jacob *(perhaps in a dream state)*. This was the blessing, but Jacob couldn't recognize the God inside of himself, because Jacob couldn't see what God saw. God saw Himself ameliorating the spirit of man to receive His true image as the likeness, resemblance, a true depiction of the representation and stature that God had created in the beginning of the creation of this world.

Jacob's visibility of God was seeing himself as God's Spirit in the flesh as a change agent that God worked through for revision, and Jacob had been revised and encouraged, for he had never experienced the spirit of God like this before and knew that something had been given, a reflection or contemplation of God's image in himself, the true brokenness of a fragile humus body. Peniel became an altar of remembrance of the encounter with the Spirit of God and God's invisibility to interact with the humus temple that is His creative glory.

In trying to give reference to the invisible nature of Yahweh, once again, the references have to come from the Pentateuch scripture (First five books of the Hebrew bible) of the true Hebrew Bible, which precludes the nature of what God's invisible substance is to the humus creature and how the prophets would receive the true message from Yahweh of His image. Here, we visit the book of *Isaiah 6:1-6*, the prophet giving a vision from God Most High:

"In the year of King Uzziah's death, I saw the Lord sitting on a throne, lofty and exalted, with the train of His robe filling the temple."

"Seraphim stood above Him, each having six wings; with two, he covered his face, and with two he covered his feet, and with two he flew."

"And one called out to another and said, "Holy, Holy, Holy, is the Lord of hosts, the whole earth is full of His glory."

"And the foundations of the thresholds trembled at the voice of him who called out, while the temple was filling with smoke"

"Then I said, "Woe is me, for I am ruined! Because I am a man of unclean lips, and I live among a people of unclean lips; for my eyes have seen the King, the Lord of hosts."

"Then one of the seraphim flew to me, with a burning coal in his hand, which he had taken from the altar with tongs."

As visuals would have it, we must deal with the statement made earlier, *"nothing is more difficult than to divert the mind from the habit of reliance on the eyes, educated and uneducated alike, from the erroneous habit of theological anthropomorphism- that is, imagining divinity in human form."*

Deffinbaugh makes this statement,

"Isaiah most certainly saw the God of Israel, and it had a tremendous impact on him. But what do we know about how God looks from this passage? How would you describe God based upon Isaiah's description of Him? Isaiah himself has more to say about the appearance of the angels than about the appearance of God. God was seated on a throne, and He wore a robe. The angels did not proclaim what God looked like, but what He was like."

They proclaimed the character of God. They spoke of His holiness and of His glory. The impact on Isaiah was an enhanced awareness of his wretchedness as a sinner. This revelation of God's character caused Isaiah to see how woefully short of God's glory, he fell. As Isaiah grew in his knowledge of the character of God, he grew in his knowledge of himself. The picture Isaiah saw of himself was not pretty."

This is a similar situation we find ourselves in today, different times, but the same place that Isaiah found himself turned inside out by self-confidence, lack of wisdom, and in need of the true wisdom that would have to come from Yahweh. Deffinbaugh goes on to explain,

"In those instances where men are said to have seen God, surprise is expressed that they lived to tell about it. Jacob marveled that his life had been preserved" (Gen. 32:30). In the New Testament, the Apostle Paul seems to be saying that men and women cannot see God and live when he declares that God dwells in unapproachable light" (1 Tim. 6:16).

The Seraphim Angels are the angel-like creatures that protect the entrance to the throne of God. Dionysius, the Areopagite who believed Paul and followed Paul's teachings (Acts 17:34), describes them: "In this form of fiery serpents, it is said that the light they give off is so intense, that not even other divine beings may look upon them. There are said to be four of these angelic beings.

They are listed as the four holy beasts in the book of revelation and are also described as angels with four faces and six wings."

This detailed enumeration of the Seraphim angel enlightens us about a creature that is said to have these qualities of brilliant light that protects the entrance where God resides. This supports Paul's comments that man cannot see God and live, that He dwells in unapproachable light. Isaiah's depiction of the Seraphim *(**Isaiah. 6:2**)* that stood above him indicates that this light is unapproachable. Isaiah stands as a credible witness based on the epilogues that support his visions. Our visions in this life seem to come into alignment with what Isaiah speaks; these visions and dreams have a tremendous impact on all of God's creation.

Chapter 2
Does God Choose to Remain Invisible?

So as we look into our next thought, the question that comes to mind is, does God want to be seen by His creatures? The name Yahweh has been removed from modern-day religions; most believers call on the name of God, Jesus, or depending on their culture, it may be many other names. The Hebrew Jews of the Old Testament used this name "YHWH" seldom because of its holiness. In our current world situation, man has tried to reverse the tide of Yahweh's victorious nature, His ability to deliver His chosen remnant from the spoils of an evil worldview environment produced by His creatures, who have turned their backs on Him and desire to worship false deities. This is the peculiar mixture of Clans, sin, and debauchery that clouds the invisible nature of Yahweh.

Have we set a tide of deception in communication that has excluded Yahweh's invisibility from being present in our midst? How long must we, in our humus nature, suffer while those who hold the true artifacts and principles of the triune God-YHWH-Creator use this name to suppress and oppressor to keep the Spirit of YHWH invisible from connecting with His glorious creation? We must call out HIS Glorious name in great power even in the midst of our oppressors! In an online journal called *"The Name Our Teachers Have Taught Us To Forget,"* the writer investigates the name, Yahweh:

> *"The Name of Yahweh does not call us; in fact, Yahweh's Name is not even uttered, because we have been taught that it is not acceptable to do so. We are taught that we must not pronounce the Holy Name of our Creator and Father, Yahweh, the Name the chosen of Yahweh will be known by, the Name those who are delivered will call upon! Our teachers instruct us that Yahweh's Name is too holy to pronounce; therefore, we are to call Him "Adonai"(Master, Lord) and "Elohim" (God inside Jesus)."*

> *"This teaching has been fully ingrained in the minds of nearly all Israelites to the point that extreme hatred is shown toward anyone who openly speaks or writes the one and only true Name of the Creator. Remember this, because the holy prophets both spoke and wrote the true Name. As a result, the Name of Yahweh has almost been forgotten (in effect, profaned or brought to*

nothing), and Baal's name is remembered and proclaimed worldwide." Yahweh.com

As we will read from authoritative sources, there was a time when the Name Yahweh was pronounced by all of Yahweh's people in prayers, blessings, and in greetings. However, by the third century B.C.E., our teachers began teaching that Yahweh, the true Name of our Creator, was too holy to pronounce. This teaching is a practice that was not inspired by our Father but one that gradually came about due to pagan influence.

At first, the practice was to pronounce the name Adonai instead of the Name Yahweh wherever Yahweh's Name was written in the Holy Scriptures. However, as time went on, changes were made to the original writings. Vowel points (which were not originally part of the text) were added to Yahweh's Name, causing the reader to pronounce the names Adonai and Elohim instead, and in many places, these alternate names were actually written in place of Yahweh's Name altogether. I'll show you the many sources verifying these facts, but *The Encyclopedia Judaica,* Volume 7, pages 680-682, sums it up rather well, as you can see for yourself.

> *"YHWH. The personal name of the God of Israel is written in the Hebrew Bible with the four consonants yhwh and is referred to as the "Tetragrammaton." At least*

until the destruction of the First Temple in 586 B.C.E., this name was regularly pronounced with its proper vowels, as is clear from the Lachish Letters, written shortly before that date.

But at least by the third century b.c.e., the pronunciation of the name YHWH was avoided, and Adonai, "the Lord "was substituted for it, as evidenced by the use of the Greek word Kyrios, "Lord," for YHWH in the Septuagint, the translation of the Hebrew Scriptures that was begun by Greek-speaking Jews in that century. Where the combined form Adonai YHWH occurs in the Bible, this was read as Adonai Elohim, "Lord God. "

In the early Middle Ages, when the consonantal text of the Bible was supplied with vowels points to facilitate its correct traditional reading, the vowel points for 'Adonai with one variation – a sheva with the first yod of YHWH instead of the hataf-patah under the aleph of 'Adona' were used for YHWH, thus producing the form Yahweh.

> *When Christian scholars of Europe first began to study Hebrew, they did not understand what this really meant, and they introduced the hybrid name "Jehovah." In order to avoid pronouncing even the sacred name Adonai for YHWH, the custom was later introduced of saying simply in Hebrew ha-Shem (or Aramaic Shemc, "the Name") even in such an expression as "Blessed be he that cometh in the name of YHWH" (Ps. 118:26).*

The prohibition applies both to the pronunciation of the name of God and its commitment to writing, apart from its use in sacred writings. The prohibition against the pronunciation of the name of God applies only to the Tetragrammaton, which could be pronounced by the high priest only once a year on the Day of Atonement in the Holy of Holies (cf. Mishnah Yoma 6:2) and in the Temple by the priests when they recited the Priestly Blessings (Sot. 7:6; see also Ch. Albeck (ed.), Seder Nashim (1954), 387). As the Talmud expresses it: *"Not as I am written am I pronounced. I am written yod he vav he, and I am pronounced alef dalet"* (nun yod, i.e., Adonai; Kid. 71a). Yahweh.com

In ancient times, the Hebrew words were written without vowels in what is called the unpointed script, so each word consists of a group of consonants whose vowel sounds were supplied from memory by the reader. In other words,

Hebrew words were pronounced with vowel sounds even though the vowels themselves were not written. The Hebrews knew, from oral teaching and practice, which vowels were associated with the different words. Yahweh's Name is written *yod-heh-waw-heh* יהוה in Hebrew, transliterated YHWH in English, but written and pronounced with the proper vowels YAHWEH as these sources show. Notice what *the Jewish Encyclopedia* of 1901, Volume 12, page 119, states:

> "It thus becomes <u>possible to determine with a fair degree of certainty the historical pronunciation of the Tetragrammaton</u>, the results agreeing with the statement of Ex. iii. 14, in which <u>YHWH</u> terms Himself. אהיה <u>"I will be,"</u> a phrase, which is immediately preceded by the fuller term "<u>I will be that I will be</u>" or, as in the English versions, "<u>I am</u>" and "<u>I am that I am</u>." The name is accordingly derived from the root הוה (= היה) and is regarded as an imperfect. <u>This passage is decisive for the pronunciation "Yahweh" for the etymology was undoubtedly based on the known word.</u>"

Esoteric purpose is the key element that is posed on the children of Israel to fashion the age-old tradition (speaking the name Yahweh) that is conducted in secrecy by the Most High Priest once a year during that time frame. This was done to acknowledge that there were no other gods worthy to receive the name above all names during these periods of B.C. and during the first half of the first century. Then again, maybe they knew the power of this name and didn't want to share the names.

There were variations mentioned towards how to pronounce the name of Yahweh, but as time lingered on, the emphasis was dropped, and in modern times, the name of the God of Israel is addressed as common wordplay in most churches as a signification of grandeur amongst preachers and ministers whose sole purpose is to entertain the masses. Just as Yahweh removed His Spirit from the temple during the time in which Israel was committing sins against Yahweh, as a form of pride and self-shame, we're seeing the same results play out today based on the selfless worship going on throughout the world.

It would be safe to say that Yahweh isn't showing Himself in our midst because we're not showing ourselves in this realm that we really are Yahweh's people; we are blind guides and can't see ourselves, and therefore, we can't see the visible nature of Yahweh amongst us. Perhaps we should invest our thoughts as to why Yahweh would make Himself invisible.

In an article posted online about why God exists, the writer (who is unknown) has a sound discussion about their thoughts as it relates to this possibility:

"Our belief in God is often described as something that we can just see plainly as a consequence of the existence of the world,

for it is obviously not rational to believe that nothing created everything. When speaking of our knowledge of Christ, the inerrancy of Scripture and so forth, we might appeal to the internal witness of the Holy Spirit, that we know that God has revealed himself to mankind in the Scripture because he has revealed himself to us on a personal level."

We know the Lord as we might know another human being. I would say that these are the most usual epistemological sources for certainty of Christian theology. But we might ask, why are they even necessary? If God were visible, we would not need them. Therefore, the question that arises is, why is God invisible?"

"While many philosophers recognize that it is possible to reason to the conclusion that God exists by way of forensic evidence, we still ponder why we need forensic evidence at all. Why does God not just make himself known to all people of the world, declaring with booming voices across the sky that Jesus Christ is Lord? Why not hover in the sky crossed arms for the entire world to see as they look up into the sky? Well, the immediate answer would be that God is immaterial and a

spatial, and therefore could not be contained by the material and spatial world."

"However, he could still manifest himself in some way that is visible to all people at all times, even if God in his fullness could not necessarily be revealed to us in that way. This is something that is consistent with the Bible, in that it tells us in 1 John 4:12 that nobody has ever seen God. But why is that? Why is God invisible?"

"At face value, it may seem as though God being visible to all people would help to achieve his end since it would certainly make everybody aware of his existence. Indeed if God's goal is to make all of mankind aware of his existence, booming voices across the sky or some sort of visible manifestation would be quite effective. The problem, though, is that God's goal is not to bring people into knowledge of his existence."

"As Romans 1:20 tells us, "For since the creation of the world God's invisible qualities—his eternal power and divine nature—have been clearly seen, being understood from what has been made, so that people are without excuse."

"The Bible tells us that God has left sufficient forensic evidence for us to believe that he exists, so that is not his goal for mankind. But rather, God's goal for mankind is for us to come into a loving relationship with him freely. In light of this goal, there is no reason to think that a visible manifestation or booming voices across the sky would serve any function. Showing people that God exists may be of no effect in bringing them into a loving relationship with him. They may just not want him either way."

"This can be demonstrated in that many people do believe that God exists, in fact, know that he exists, and yet are not in a relationship with him because it is not what they want for their lives. From this, I think it follows that assuring men of God's existence may not necessarily draw people freely into a relationship with him, and therefore there is just no reason for God to reveal himself in that way. So would visibility make people aware of his existence? Yes. But making people aware of his existence is not God's goal."

"It may even be argued that visibility would have a negative effect on bringing people into a loving relationship with God on their own accord. If God were hovering in the sky, men might feel as they were being compelled to act in a certain way and

being stripped of their autonomy. Something like how teenagers become angry and rebel in response to overwhelming parental strictures."

"In this way, visibility may bring people further away from a relationship with God, even if it makes them aware of his existence. This is a behavior that we see all of the time in children and anybody who is forced into a situation where there is an overwhelming and overriding authority. Our society would be radically different from what it is now, and far from guaranteeing that men would behave better, I submit that many would display conduct that is even more depraved than what is now present."

"Therefore the argument against God's existence from invisibility cannot stand firmly against scrutiny for two reasons,

1. *God's goal is not to make men aware of his existence, so visibility would have no function.*
2. *It may be the case that visibility would have a negative effect on mans' relationship with God.*

"For this reason, as a logical argument against the existence of God, this does not really threaten anything, and as a purely

intellectual question for Christians to ponder, I think the answers I have provided are quite sufficient." Jim Boucher

This article supports the thought that Yahweh's invisible nature could be possible if Yahweh thought it necessary for man to see Him and live; however, God desires that man have life and have it more abundantly with the signs that exist in the landscape that stands before us (all infused matter), as faith is more important than sight. In other words, the invisibility of Yahweh was not as important as to be seen but to have faith that He existed in the midst of His creation.

If God were visible, what would man actually do with that? Would men have figured out another way to hide from God, or would the creatures be perfectly obedient because they would be in fear of the sight of God? In the book of Exodus, Moses is warned by God about His presence in the midst of His chosen people; the tabernacle was the meeting place between God and His creatures. This tent that they met in was the dwelling place of God, "for having God in close proximity was a very dangerous thing, when Moses pleads with God to dwell in the midst of His people" *(Exodus 34:9)*. God warned him that this could prove fatal to such a sinful people: "For the Lord had said to Moses, Say to the sons of Israel, ***"You are an obstinate people; should I go up in your midst for one moment, I would destroy you"***
-Exodus 33:5

Being in the midst of Yahweh was a powerful and overwhelming situation for the Israelites, as their only refuge was the tabernacle, which was the tent that separated them from the sight of God. They weren't allowed to enter into the

holy of holies due to the dwelling of God's spirit; upon seeing this, it was said that they would die. So does this mean that, if we see God, we must die? Well, yes, the only way to approach Yahweh is that we must be outside our bodies, and that's a fact. The scripture lines this up in the second book of Corinthians:
"We are confident, I say and would prefer to be away from the body and at home with the Lord"
- *2 Corinthians 5:8*

Maybe this is how God has lined this up: While we are in our dirt sanctuary that houses His spirit, He remains invisible until we depart from our earthly bodies, but we must also realize that God desires that we understand the power that HE has as the creator of a vast universe. We can't comprehend this vastness, and we must understand He has placed Himself in the vastness of His creation to work out a plan that He has placed in the Word. Although it is complex, God came back in the flesh, full of power as the Son of man, to show those in a future time His plan for His created creatures.

As we move forward, how should we view ourselves from the perspective of being in dirt bodies with a spirit? In relation to how we have been taught to think, this is thought-provoking, to say the least, how we view God's invisibility as it relates to us. This question becomes relevant based on our position as creatures in the vast anomaly of God's provisions. This in part, becomes the visible conception of His dominion that is right before our eyes. What we should see about God's viability is in the form of His invisibility. In an article written by Jud Davis, he interprets the thoughts of an Epicurus nature in modern times, and the relationship to what God has proven in the mindset of a literal position, wherein God reveals himself through the believer who finds faith as the catalyst of revelations of HIS existence in the creation of His creature.

> *"Romans 1:18–21 has a more direct answer to modern Epicurus. Those who have never heard are willfully guilty for rejecting God because God has revealed Himself clearly in the wonders of creation."*

> *"When we witness to people, we don't have to worry about proving God's existence. According to this verse, God makes Himself evident, open, and plain to everyone. He literally placed the evidence in them. Apparently, God placed the knowledge of Himself within all men—inside their minds, in their hearts, in the very core of their being.*

> *"The verb is present tense. God did not reveal Himself in the past and then stop. He continues to reveal Himself within us now."*

> *"So, when people like Epicurus try to appease their conscience and justify their sin, they must suppress their knowledge of God. They grab at straws to patch together a cage around the*

truth. But God's truth breaks free, like a tiger ill-suited for captivity."

"The King of Heaven does not rely on petty heralds to share who He is. Nor does He post little notes on bulletin boards, hoping we'll see them. God, Himself takes a personal interest in making sure that each one of us has knowledge of Him."

"God knows that all people fight against this knowledge. Jesus could tell everyone what He once said to Saul, a zealous Pharisee, **"It is hard for you to kick against the pricks"** **(Acts 9:5)**. He pricks every heart, letting each person know about Him".

"For his invisible attributes are thoroughly known from the creation of the cosmos, being known by means of the things which have been made, whether his eternal power or divinity... (Romans 1:20a)"

"What can we see about God? His invisible attributes! The Greek verb kathoratai intensifies the standard Greek word meaning "to see." So we don't merely "see" God's attributes, but we literally see them "down" to the core. We clearly perceive, we abundantly know, we thoroughly recognize God's *invisible attributes. Poor Epicurus was just bluffing. Everyone sees God clearly, even if they never saw a Bible or heard about Him."*

"God reveals Himself in two ways. One is through the special revelation of the Bible. God also communicates through the "general" revelation of creation. While it does not replace the saving truths that mankind must learn in the Bible, creation clearly teaches all men and women that God exists and that certain things are true about Him."

"We know these things presently and continually. The moment God created the world (cosmos in Greek), His world began proclaiming things about the Creator, and it has continued ever since."

"Romans 1:20 spells out the attributes that we can see in the world—God's eternal nature and divine power. The Greek word for eternal, "a-i-di-os," is unusual. It is related to the Greek word meaning "always." God has caused an "always-ness" to be evident in the created order, and people connect this "always-ness" with the idea of a personal God." Jud Davis

In order for God to have aidios (eternal), this alwaysness is presence as a transcending characteristic of the spirit based on God always being. This could spell out that Yahweh's invisible nature is the spirit of man, and while in this dirt body, we take on the appearance of the world in which the humus was formed and houses the spirit of God as it transcends through its journey on earth. The spirit is invisible, but the flesh shows a pictorial representation of our worldly appearance and characteristics, the invisibility of God as the spirit desires that the flesh conforms, but the flesh is not the nature of the spirit; that's why the flesh must return to the ground from which it was formed.

The spirit is the invisible transcendence of God. It reflects the resembling nature of God and the incarnation of who the Son of man is and who the Son of God is. God transcended in the body of Christ to provide all his creatures a witness that He lives in His creation and desires HIS Spirit to transcend, embodied as a measure of proof to the multitudes that His eternal spirit is present in all creation. This representation comes as Jesus the Son (The Humus body) conformed to the Spirit of God that incarnated His Holy (whole) body, being one with God. This is no mystery but something that the humus creature must engage in to understand the invisibility of the spirit inside; it has been placed in us to praise and transcend.

In an article written by John Piper, he explains this attribute relating to the image of God based on a Christian's belief. In this article, John Piper engages in detail the image presented of God's spiritual manifestation in the flesh and the invisibility of God's presence,

> *"We are now in a position to ask what the author of Genesis 1:26, 27; 5:1, 2; and 9:6 really intended to convey about the image of God in man. To answer this, let us observe more closely the context of Genesis one. What features of the creation narrative are unique to man?*
>
> 1. *Man is the final creation.*
> 2. *Only man is stated as being in the image of God.*
> 3. *Only man is given dominion over all the earth.*
> 4. *Prior to the creation of man, man alone, was there divine counsel?*
> 5. *Only man is explicitly stated as being created, male and female. Now what, if anything, does each of these features contribute to our understanding of God's image in man?*
>
> *First, that man was the final creation gives rise to such statements, as "Man is the crown of creation, the end toward which it was all directed." But this tells us nothing about the nature of God's image.*

> *Second, and by far the most important feature of Genesis one, is the actual statement that man is in God's image. On the basis of the linguistic evidence presented above, it would reflect a theological prejudice to deny that the author means man's physical appearance images his Maker."*

As Von Rad states,

> *"The marvel of man's bodily appearance is not at all to be accepted from the realm of God's image. This was the original notion, and we have no reason to suppose that it completely gave way, in Paul's theological reflection, to a spiritualizing and intellectualizing tendency. Therefore, one will do well to split the physical from the spiritual as little as possible: the whole man is created in God's image."*

> *As we ponder this notion, we must ask ourselves a serious question, "Why are we here?" "Throughout my life we've listened and wondered what this life is really all about, in retrospect, we didn't realize this, but we the creatures who are placed here on earth to carry the light placed in us, we are to break the curses of a broken kingdom and restore its true values; we transcend time as truth-bearers in a dirt body."*

We should believe the human condition is a fascinating journey; however, the syndrome that we are born into allows the humus creature the opportunity to adapt and evolve past the philosophical, political pragmatism, and religious theoretical dogmas presented. A lesson to all whose spirits cover the face of this reality we call life, we should understand that purpose was given in us from the divine presence of The Most High Yahweh. Without creation, there would be a vacancy sign that could be seen from the heavens that reads, "No image available." Without God, man cannot, and without man, God will not; He needs you, His creation on earth, just as he proposed in scripture: **"And God said, let us make man in our image, after our likeness: and let them have dominion over the fish of the sea, and over the fowl of the air, and over the cattle, and overall the earth, and every creeping thing that creepeth upon the earth -Gen. 1:26-28**, as stated in the paragraph above,

> *"Man is the crown of creation, the end toward which it was all directed." The light-infused justification that moves us through this life comes with an insurance policy that states this, as long as this model called the humus body is used according to the light specifications in which it is intended, it carries a lifelong warranty, not only in its use in this lifetime, but the eternal life to come, in other words, if you follow this warranty you can rest assured this product will never wear*

out, but be renewed in the eternal life to come. If you have any questions relating to this humus model, please consult and read the covenants of holy scripture that spells out all of its terms and conditions. Please use this warranty accordingly while on earth in your dirt body with a spirit. Please enjoy your time on earth with Yahweh' product...The Humus Body.

"We are hard pressed on every side, but not crushed; perplexed, but not in despair;

Persecuted, but not abandoned; struck down, but not destroyed.

We always carry around in our bodies the death of Jesus so that the life of Jesus may also be revealed in our body.

For we who are alive are always being given over to death for Jesus' sake, so that his life may also be revealed in our mortal body.

So then, death is at work in us, but life is at work in you"

-2 Cor. 4:8-12

Chapter 3

The Spiritual Incarnation of Yahweh

At this point, Yahweh's invisibility places Himself in the midst of the creature and in the image of the human creature, but what about the spiritual incarnation of God in a man? Is this the part that has been forfeited? Have we allowed our image, character, and integrity to be seized by the barbaric nature of clan leaders throughout the world? This isn't God's design or His will, but it is our will outside of Yahweh's Kingdom. Adam died; Christ ascended. The spark of invisibility should be our consummation in Yahweh invisibility.

Those who trust the invisibility in Jesus should feel this way and not apart in the love that God has for the totality of His creation; we are all called Christians per say, and Christianity is not part of the total game, and its rules don't exist in modern society. The aim is to be "One" in the trinity. Being one with God means to be "Holy." The Lord our God is one, and so is His creation. There shouldn't be any substitutions for the plans that God has for His people. We follow the laws of God; in this, we don't have to be policed.

The cultural elite does not have the power to deconstruct the holiness of the Kingdom of God. Their conspiracies only play into the prophecies of the scriptures where God will use evil to bring about righteousness; Christendom has brought about the truth of man's heart, but ultimately, every knee shall bow, and every tongue will confess.

Will we have to wait for this as a future transformation? John Piper touches on this matter as well, as he writes in this article:

> *"In the New Testament, the primary word for "image" is* eikōn. *Secondary words are* homosiōsis *and* charaktēr. *Eikōn appears in twenty verses throughout the New Testament. In twelve of these, it explicitly denotes physical representations. In one verse, it refers to the Law as not being the true image of things to come (Hebrews 10:1). Twice it is used to denote Christ as the image of God (2 Corinthians 4:4, Colossians 1:15), and five times it relates man to the image of*

Christ or God (Romans 8:29, 1 Corinthians 11:7, 15:49, 2 Corinthians 3:18, Colossians 3:10). James uses homosiōsis, *saying that men "are made in the* likeness of God" *(James 3:9). The author of the epistle to the Hebrews uses* character *to say that Christ is the express* representation *of God's nature (Hebrews 1:3)."*

"In the New Testament, Jesus Christ is the image of God, and when all the information is gathered, we know we are speaking of "image" here in a radically different sense than we found in the Old Testament. "He is the image of the invisible God.... For in him all the fullness of God was pleased to dwell" (Colossians 1:15, 19; cf. 2 Corinthians 4:4). Concerning our image, it sounds as if we as God's creation were made in His image and given His spirit, but based on the fall of Adam the spirit had been diminished, and a more perfect image of us outside of the image of Adam was being redefined through Jesus Christ."

"The men who saw Jesus Christ saw God (John 12:45, 14:9). Jesus is the effulgence of God's glory and the representation of his very nature (Hebrews 1:3, John 1:14). Now, if Christ is the

image of God, in what sense does the New Testament see man as being in God's image?"

"In the fifteenth chapter of 1 Corinthians, verses 35 to 50 answers the questions, "How are the dead raised? With what kind of body do they come?" (v. 35) After discussing in detail the resurrection of the dead, Paul gives the summary statement: "And as we have borne the image of the earthy, we shall also bear the image of the heavenly" (verse 49, ASV). The context makes it clear that Paul is thinking in personal terms: Adam is earthy, and Christ is heavenly.

We must ask what the "image of the heavenly" involves. The answer is found in noting what specifics verse 49 summaries. The "image of the heavenly" has to do with the nature of the resurrection body. "It is sown in corruption; it is raised in incorruption: it is sown in dishonor; it is raised in glory: it is sown in weakness; it is raised in power; it is sown a natural body; it is raised a spiritual body" (vv. 42-44, ASV). Thus. to take on the 'image of the heavenly" is to be incorruptible, glorious, powerful, and spiritual."

In this understanding presented by John Piper, we must look at the invisibility of God as the coming of His glorious appearance. We will be made aware that inside our physical body is the spirit of Yahweh. The outcomes that are in store of the visible manifestation of God are in us as a spiritual reflection; this shall be seen in glorious nature, and our earthly bodies will be consumed by our heavenly bodies. The invisible will become visible through "The Son of God."

In this exposition, we read about the image of God in Christ and in man. There seems to be a further understanding that should be acknowledged; not only is the image of God given, but also the character of God is given in Christ, and the crowning glory of the three was the integrity of God. Character and integrity are interrelated in the trinity as an inherent character trait within the Father.

Our invisible character should exhibit the obedience and practices that were the foundational ethical precepts of Yahweh's Word. The integrity portion in the invisibility of the light given should produce the kingdom values that Jesus added to the twelve disciples whose testimonies later resonated throughout the New Testament. These character traits were given to offset the deceptions presented by Satan through man's lack of understanding and greed as it relates to power, money, and the flesh. Our image, character, and integrity given in Christ were to galvanize our spirit to overcome the powers in this worldly system in that of a forfeited nature of fallen man. As we're sown in corruption, we've raised in corruption. This is the truth in following what is embedded in us while in the world and then what is manifested in us as the image of God. We are in this world but not of this world.

CHAPTER 4

THE INVISIBILITY IN JESUS CHRIST (YESHUA HAMASCHIACH)

What is the invisibility nature of God in Jesus that actually shows the visible nature of God? In the book of Colossians, the passage states: *"The Son is the image of the invisible God, the firstborn over all creation"-Colossians 1:15 (NIV),*
and in the book of John, it was demonstrated this way, *"In the beginning was the Word, and the Word was with God, and the Word was God."-John 1:1 (NIV).*

Before we take a deeper dive into the onset of the invisibility of Jesus Christ, let's ask ourselves a few pertinent questions,

What do we really know about the Son of God in the name of Jesus Christ?

Where did this name come from?

Where was it designated in history, and why has man taken this name "Jesus" and placed it as a badge of honor, a name above all names?

Well, there is another name of the Messiah that is reflective of the name Jesus Christ, which is hidden from the biblical reference and is unknown to many Christians; this name, Yeshua HaMashiach is a mystery.

The Hebrew term Mashiach (or Messiah in English; Cristos, or Christ, in Greek) means "anointed one" and refers to a person who was set apart to serve Yahweh.

In the Old Testament, God's Mashiachs were anointed with oil to symbolize the presence and authority of the Holy Spirit (Leviticus 4:3, 1 Samuel 12:14, 2 Samuel 19:21).

God promised Israel an ultimate Mashiach, or Messiah, and gave over 300 prophecies regarding the "Anointed One" so that they would recognize Him when He came (Isaiah 53:1, Psalm 22:27, 10:1-4, Daniel 9:25, 7:1). Jesus fulfilled every one of them, thus deserving the title Yeshua Hamaschiach for the Jewish people. However, Jesus came into the world to offer salvation and forgiveness to everyone who calls upon His name (John 3:16–18, Acts 2:21). Surrounding His throne for all eternity will be people from "every nation, tribe, and tongue" (Revelation 7:9). God is not offended by our language or our differences.

Throughout the Bible, Yahweh even identified Himself by different names as He dealt with people in different ways (Exodus 3:14, Isaiah 48:12, Revelation 1:8). Jesus called Himself the "Son of Man" (Matthew 26:24, Luke 22:22), and others called Him "Teacher" (Matthew 8:19) and "Rabbi" (John 1:49). He never once corrected anyone's pronunciation or use of a messianic title, as long as the person came to Him in faith. Therefore, the name we use for the Son of God (when we come to Him in faith) appears to be unimportant to Him. He hears our hearts, regardless of the words our mouths are speaking (Luke 9:47).

In the words of Dr. Brown,

"Do not be ashamed to use the name JESUS!"

That is the proper way to say his name in English—just as Michael is the correct

English way to say the Hebrew name mi-kha-el and Moses is the correct English way to say the Hebrew name mo-sheh. Pray in Jesus' name, worship in Jesus' name, and witness in Jesus' name. And for those who want to relate to our Messiah's Jewishness, then refer to him by His original name Yeshua—not Yahshua and not Yahushua—remembering that the power of the name is not in its pronunciation but in the person to whom it refers, our Lord and Redeemer and King."

We can also point out a significant theological nugget as it relates to the invisibility of God's physical being, versus an invisible image. We can engage a vital complexity of the invisibility of God. Yahweh is and has always shown His invisible nature throughout the OT as the living God of all nations.

Dr. Myles Monroe made this observation,

> "Vision without values is destiny without discipline. What have we done? Vision is the Source and hope of life. The greatest gift ever given to mankind is not the gift of sight, but the gift of vision. Sight is a function of the eyes; vision is a function of the heart. 'Eyes that look are common, but eyes that see are rare. "Nothing noble or noteworthy on earth was ever done without vision."

Unfortunately, we are operating as stooges in their remedial religious and social systems. Now let's challenge this thought… let us look at our irremediable behaviors as societies in this world.

- We are messengers sent into the world for the sole purpose of witnessing and build upon the power that Yahweh has placed in us.
- We are being influenced by the unnatural or fallen spirits of a displaced spiritual realm that is lower in its principals than what God has purposed it.

His creation through salvation is to minister through the kingdom spirit to bring out those who are worshiping in their sins. Maybe, just maybe, Yahweh is waging war against this world based on the Baal worship that has been instituted into our realm of worship for centuries. We may be calling out the name of demonic forces that bring glory to Satan and his fallen Imp creatures that are honoring evil in our world. God is a jealous God who will not share His Glory with another. *"You must worship no other gods, for the LORD, whose very name is Jealous, is a God who is jealous about his relationship with you."*

Fact check, this message was given unto us, but was it given to protect the sanctity of their gods and their form of worship in this realm? What is the harm if we, as the Most High creation, challenge the broken systems of this world? (Check your world history and biblical facts). These systems have been in place for centuries, and we've remained in them as subjects or underlings. We are the remnant, the totality of The Most High royalty. Yahweh's truth should be spoken, not that of a sanctioned supremacy.

The names of Yahweh are beyond our imagination, so what about these names that are rarely used? Are there other hidden names that are kept from the populous of the world cultures?

- *El Shaddai (Lord God Almighty)*
- *El Elyon (The Most High God)*

- *Adonai (Lord, Master)*
- *Yahweh (Lord, Jehovah)*
- *Jehovah Nissi (The Lord My Banner)*
- *Jehovah-Raah (The Lord My Shepherd)*
- *Jehovah Rapha (The Lord That Heals)*
- *Jehovah Shammah (The Lord Is There)*
- *Jehovah Tsidkenu (The Lord Our Righteousness)*
- *Jehovah Mekoddishkem (The Lord Who Sanctifies You)*
- *El Olam (The Everlasting God)*
- *Elohim (God)*
- *Qanna (Jealous)*
- *Jehovah Jireh (The Lord Will Provide)*
- *Jehovah Shalom (The Lord Is Peace)*
- *Jehovah Sabaoth (The Lord of Hosts)*

This impermeant realm that we are living in is filled with God's Glory. Our flesh is organic, and it will return to the organic state (the humus dirt), but our spirit, well, it is everlasting. It is eternally gifted to transcend time and space. The demonic influences that are grounded in this mindset here on earth are in lust with this style of living. They cannot effectively imagine the kingdom of God and all its natural qualities. The grounded ones are sold to the prince of this air (hierarchies of the kingdoms on earth) to receive all that this world has to offer, and this is okay; however, we must remember that we are the created of Yahweh, and we must honor this invisible nature before all creation.

Remember when Satan offered Jesus all his kingdoms of this world and its splendor? If Jesus had bowed down and worshiped Satan, we all would be in the same mindset. Instead, Jesus made a bold, everlasting, and firm statement to the evil one, *"Away from me, Satan! For it is written, Worship the Lord your God, and serve Him only."* This metaphorical passage gives believers the same will as their creator to transcend in the eternal realm with endless possibilities here on earth.

Many of creation is blind, just as Saul was when he meshed into the religious beliefs and traditions that he had been taught throughout his life as a Pharisee. He was sold to the spirits of this world. Saul made up his mind that it was better to kill Christians than to let them worship in the name of Jesus. Saul wasn't torn between what was right or what was wrong; he was sold on what he had been taught as a Pharisee in the Jewish tradition and by practicing the discriminating principles the devil embedded in his mind. His only course of reasoning was tradition and culture through education. There was nothing challenging before the Jewish councils and nothing after it, according to Saul and his counterparts. They had created their own rules and laws to challenge institutions outside their reasoning and traditions.

"The Pharisees and teachers of the law said to Jesus, "Your followers don't follow the traditions we have from our great leaders who lived long ago. They eat their food with hands that are not clean. Why do they do this?"

Jesus answered, "You are all hypocrites. Isaiah was right when he wrote these words from God about you: 'These people honor me with their words, but I am not really important to them.

Their worship of me is worthless. The things they teach are only human rules."

You have stopped following God's commands, preferring instead the man-made rules you got from others."

Then he said, "You show great skill in avoiding the commands of God so that you can follow your own teachings!

Moses said, 'You must respect your father and mother. He also said, 'Whoever says anything bad to their father or mother must be killed.

But you teach that people can say to their father or mother, 'I have something I could use to help you, but I will not use it for you. I will give it to God.

You are telling people that they do not have to do anything for their father or mother.

So you are teaching that it is not important to do what God said. You think it is more important to follow those traditions you have, which you pass on to others. And you do many things like that."

Jesus called the people to him again. He said, "Everyone should listen to me and understand what I am saying.

There is nothing people can put in their mouth that will make them wrong. People are made wrong by what comes from inside them." -Mark 7:5-16 (ERV)

Now here stands a similar behavioral pattern of Saul in modern times. The people in this day and age are dedicated to a form of religion they don't understand. Christians, in general, are so protective of this form of religion that most are willing to go into the ground with it. We have been taught this form of religion so it can keep us sinning within its confines, which allows its prey the comfort of feeling safe within those boundaries.

For example, we worship on Sunday and, without reason, become angry while in worship and remain angry when we come out of it. You want to know why? Because many are operating in the unknown! Having a smile on your face while listening to a sermon doesn't mean you're enjoying its meaning. In fact, the Holy Spirit is rejecting the mistrust, but the flesh is representing the worldly view, and by the time we reach our cars, all types of spirits have leaped on the Believer. Just like Saul, what he thought was right, what he practiced his whole life, was a tradition that had been instilled in him. He was living in the form of sin until the righteousness of Christ found him and pricked him with the Truth.

This type of Truth only took a moment to change Saul because "the Truth" threw out all the polluted worship that he had been trained in for years. Our mindset is very similar to Saul's because we, too are carrying years of garbage in our minds. We've been trained to follow the traditions of a broken society. Well, fellow Believers, it is time to rebuke this mindset that has been placed on us and grab hold of the Kingdom Gospel and its principles.

Jesus described us as the salt of the earth, *"But if the salt loses its saltiness, how can it be made salty again? It is no longer good for anything except to be thrown out and trampled by men." - Matthew 5:13*

Yeshua speaks about those who hear the kingdom gospel as: *"You are the light of the world. A city on a hill cannot be hidden.*

Neither do people light a lamp and put it under a bowl. Instead, they put it on its stand, and it gives light to everyone in the house.

In the same way, let your light shine before men, that they may see your good deeds and praise your Father in heaven."
-Matthew 5:14-16

For our benefit, Angels are gathered all around us waiting for the opportunity to minister to us, although human imps are using their marching orders from Satan's lies, this leads us down the wide pathway to hell based on the errors of the scriptural passages we're taught. Thankfully, we have the power to overcome his spells, his frequencies, and his bullying nature. All we have to do is call on the Name above all names: Yahweh, Elohim, El Shaddai, Jehovah, and the devil **must** flee!

> *"The fearful durst (When something reaches a point where it is no longer enjoyable) not meet the difficulties of religion, their slavish fear came from their unbelief; but those who were so dastardly as not to dare to take up the cross of Christ, were yet so desperate as to run into abominable wickedness. The agonies and terrors of the first death will lead to the far greater terrors and agonies of eternal death."*

BH.com, Doxology, Matthew 5:17-20

God brought HIS Glory to the earth in three dimensions, Himself (El), incarnated Yeshua (Jesus), and the Holy Spirit (The Holy Ghost), each entity playing a role in time, together to increase our authority and knowledge as the humus creature. Instead of us referencing the Old Testament as Jesus did, we have looked for the easy way out; this means listening to unreliable sources.

Our world is full of information, but is it trustworthy? Now listen closely. Satan is the prince of this air. In other words, he has his system in place, and he has taken it to the airwaves. We can see this happening (by sight); he demands to have God's Kingdom. Satan has found our frequencies (our worldly desires) and has tuned us towards his bandwidth; he knows we won't read the Bible and study its true wisdom and Glory, so he preys on our ignorance.

We have been led into the feel-good know-all behavior of lesser gods (idolatry). Satan desires to have misinformed subjects to carry out his business and has found these subjects in their confused state of mind. He has manipulated our "vision" and turned us towards "television"; in other words, now Satan's television has become our truth and our vision for the future. Don't fall for it; his job is to give you the systems of this world at a price! That is, he wants to manufacture processes that you will buy into so that he owns your soul in his system!

The outcome is the fall; it's all about killing our joy, stealing our crowns, and destroying our promise of eternal life here on earth. Rebuke his system! You have been given the authority, "the spark." God's Kingdom is far superior! We are designed to operate in God's Kingdom mentality of truth and righteousness.

God said, *"Heaven and earth will pass away, but my words will never pass away."*

Now here is the Good News! All those born of God have overcome the world. Who is it that has overcome the world?

All those who believe that Jesus is the Son of God has overcome the world. We must look past systematic dictatorships and deception in religions and politics; there must be pure and Holy sanctification relating to the origins of God's true remnants.

"We know that anyone born of God does not continue to sin; the One who was born of God keeps them safe, and the evil one cannot harm them.

We know that we are children of God and that the whole world is under the control of the evil one.

We also know that the Son of God has come and has given us understanding so that we may know him who is true. And we are in him who is true by being in His Son Jesus Christ. He is the true God and eternal life.

Dear children, keep yourselves from idols." **– 1 John 5:18- 21.** Amen.

Although this may sound archaic, we all play a part in this history, and in this story, called life. I stated in the preface that cages have been placed before us. We go in and out of these cages during our lifetime, but we must realize we have the power to open and close the door to our cages. Most importantly, we are the lock and the key, so before you confine yourself to a cage, know that you have the authority to lock and unlock your confinement. Our outcomes should weld our past, current, and future postulated sequences together to develop a true perspective of events that have led us to this art that has been placed before us as literal history.

While operating in the systems of this world, we should put all our strength in God's mighty power. Put on the full armor of God so that we can and will resist the schemes of the evil one. Pray that we will recognize and discern the spiritual nature of those whose works are evil; pray and allow God to handle them.

If our faith is in Yeshua (Jesus), HE will dispatch HIS anointed in the Holy Spirit to protect us always. Remember, the Holy Spirit will not come upon a contaminated vessel, so don't be fooled by those who tell you the Holy Spirit lives in them. The Holy Spirit came upon the prophets of old and spoke to them. When this spirit of truth came, it accomplished what it had come to accomplish in all truth and righteousness. Immediately afterward, the Holy Spirit had to leave because of the realm in which man existed. This realm was and still is, contaminated.

God's creation had turned to the gods of their ancestors and worshiped idols that were outside the invisible nature of Yahweh. God will not share HIS glory with another, no wood, metal, stone, or animals. The essentials that we are to operate in consist of image, character, and integrity that are of our Creator. Our dubious behaviors blocked our truths given by the Holy Spirit. However, we should give ourselves the opportunity to regain our faith, great faith, that God has overcome this world. God has the key to this Kingdom here on earth, and we are HIS Royalty. We have the keys to this invisible Kingdom; we have King Dominion here on earth! Trust HIM. We are truly worthy of this honor.

> *"This sequence of verses (in Exodus 33) and others like in the Old Testament indicate that there was a sense in which God could not be seen at all, but there was also some outward form or manifestation of God which at least in part was to be seen by man."* 10 *The outward manifestation applies to being seen in the physical sense; that implies a spirit in a dirt body, which is what Jesus had, He was born of the flesh, (The Son) and incarnated by the Spirit (Logos) of God; Jesus was the contained light, a vessel made of dirt with the invisibility of Yahweh."*

Andrew Malone sums up the invisible image when he says,

> *"The first step is taken when we understand that the adjective 'invisible' is better understood as 'unseen.' It refers to things which are not seen, not necessarily to things which cannot be seen."*

> *"This is a brilliant interpretation of God in Jesus, the invisible nature of God is unseen, which cannot be seen by physical sight, however, aren't things that cannot be seen,*

> *but are not necessarily unseen due to its physical appearance."*

There is a term called aoratos, which came into use during the latter part of the fifth century and means invisible, or the unseen. Then there is a word termed as horatos, which means to see but to deny or refuse to acknowledge the truth or existence of what was true before the witnesses. In this case, Jesus the Messiah stood before them, but they didn't understand the physical or the intellectual. The Pharisees refused to acknowledge the truths of the flesh. They had ruled out the spiritual concept that was contained in the Torah. They didn't recognize the spirit of Jesus; instead, they found ways to deny the incarnation of God in the flesh. In this, many believers were forced to follow the negative assertions that gave way to removing God's otherness from those who witnessed the true invisibility of God in Jesus.

So, what are we to do with this? Should we throw up our hands in frustration and continue to follow the systems of the world, or should we leave these teachings handed down by our ancestors? We all are faced with decisions relating to our life and its struggles. There is one thing that has been denied over the years. This one practice that many know of, this practice has released many wise women and men from their infirmities; it's called patience! Jesus proved this throughout the scriptures.

When doubt enters our minds, we have been equipped with an invisible spark that is central to our eternity. It is probably one of the most perplexing puzzles we have ever been faced with, but this spark of light exists in the essence of God's creation. This spark enlightens us to exist, to see, to stand, to walk, to talk, to hear, to smell, to discern, to sleep, to eat, to overcome adversities, and to pray to the invisible nature of Yahweh. The created creature has not seen their creator but knows that our light is reflective of the light that is in Jesus and in the invisible nature of Yahweh.

Through patience, we summon the Holy Spirit to come into this realm. We give the Spirit of Yahweh permission to come and supp with HIS creation and to sanctify the humus creature! This is a powerful notion; God is available to HIS creation. It seems, without God, man can do nothing. By giving Yahweh permission and an invitation, HE will come and reveal HIS plans for the man/woman that HE created. He used Noah, Abraham, and Moses to accomplish his plans. All they had to do is give God permission to come into this realm. Noah gave God permission to seal the door to the ark and allow the rain to start. Abraham gave God permission to judge the cities of Sodom and Gomorrah. Moses gave Yahweh permission to part the sea and to collapse the sea. We as HIS creation have the same authority, but we must seek this authority. This is accomplished through understanding how Yahweh's Kingdom works here on earth.

"But seek ye first the Kingdom of God, and all these things shall be added unto you (Matthew 6:33)."

"Ask and it will be given to you; seek, and you will find; knock, and the door will be opened to you (Matthew 7:7)."

"For where two or three gather in my name, there am I with them (Matthew 18:20)."

Scriptures are the keys to the Kingdom of God, and we are the remnant of God Most High. It is our royal right to possess these keys, but we must first seek the truth in our hearts and minds to get to the truth on how to use these keys, and this comes from following the Kingdom Principles, the laws of Yahweh.

Chapter 5
Confidence of Light

God exists to those who believe that HE can encounter HIS creation as HE sees fit. Inside of this fleshly jumpsuit exists a Spirit that is unknown to the humus creature; his counterpart (Man) has deprived himself of such wisdom about the trueness of this invisibility of his Creator. Our position is rated by teachings presented before us and how we allow our fleshly spirit to counteract the assumptions that have been placed before us and allow the invisibility of God to supply us with truths.

In a book called *The Story of Christian Theology,* there is an example given of the apologists who explained their position as it relates to human understanding in the cultural conduct of the misinformed gentile. The apologists, who were Christian writers of the second century, were trying to influence relatively humane Roman emperors, such as Marcus Aurelius and Antonius, to take Christianity seriously, if not as true. Most of them wrote open letters to these and other emperors and officials of the Roman Empire in which they attempted to explain the truth about Christian belief and behavior, often in philosophical ways. The key to this quote is in the statement, *"They attempted to explain the truth."* To make an attempt to influence someone with different beliefs, this hinges on the fact that the (person attempted to be influenced) may have no continuity to the connections of the subject.

The apologists used a form of philosophical measures to explain something that was unexplainable,

> *"These writers were contemporaries of the Gnostics [and apostolic fathers] but took a very different path. Instead of esoteric spiritualism, the apologists confidently used philosophical reason, and though they attacked philosophers, they used their language whenever they could. They thus created the basic method of traditional Christian Theology."*

Olson Roger

Here, we find the gray matter of teaching an effectual methodology less the physiology of the incarnation properties that unite a man to God, as it relates to the invisibility of God in man. The gray matter is the unknown information (wisdom and intellect) that anthropomorphisms attempt to fill in the grey blanks (power of reasoning) about the wisdom of God. Throughout history, the early church fathers created a façade based on a story that shapes the identities of those who call themselves Christians (Followers of Christ), the distortion, and multi-vibrations (many thoughts from believers through sensory stimulation and the process of creating meaningful patterns from raw sensory information). This has created echoes of multiple factions of philosophers that have erased the invisibility and visibility of God; in other words, the true focus of the created humans and their ability to awaken to the perception of God inside themselves. This leads to the notion of God's presence on earth as an invisible source as the presence of the Holy Spirit.

There are statements that contend that God has placed reasoning before His creation concerning His invisibility, *"It seems that without God, man cannot, and without man, God will not."* –John Wesley, (Paraphrase from St. Augustine's 169th sermon). Did man create the idea of "God" and take for granted that Yahweh is the creator of the creature?

"We are a temple of God, and the Spirit of God dwells in us"
-1 Corinthians 3:16

"Our body is a temple of the Holy Spirit, which is in us because we are bought with a price. Everyone who has been purchased (Redeemed by the Spirit) by the blood of Christ also has the Spirit of God dwelling in him" -1 Corinthians 6:19

"We should be led by the Spirit of God. If the Spirit of God (Christ) does not dwell in us, we do not belong to God" - Romans 8:9

There seems to be a division amongst us humans about who we are and what we are as it relates to the natural order of the creation process. John Stott, in his article *"God invisible,"* makes a vivid statement concerning this discussion:

> *"The invisibility of God is a great problem. It was already a problem for God's people in Old Testament days. Their pagan neighbors would taunt them, saying, "Where is now your God?" Their gods were visible and tangible, but Israel's God was neither. Today in our scientific culture, young people are taught not to believe in anything, which is not open to empirical investigation. How then has God solved the problem of His own invisibility? The first answer is of course, "In Christ." Jesus Christ is the visible image of the invisible God. John 1:18: "No one has ever seen God, but God the only Son has made him known." That's wonderful," people say, but it was 2,000 years ago. Is there no way by which the invisible God makes Himself visible today? There is. We return to 1 John 4:12: "No one has ever seen God." It is precisely the same introductory statement. But instead of continuing with reference to the Son of God, it continues: "If we love one another, God*

dwells in us." In other words, the invisible God, who once made Himself visible in Christ, now makes Himself visible in Christians, if we love one another. It is a breathtaking claim. The local church cannot evangelize, proclaiming the gospel of love, if it is not itself a community of love." John Scott

In this case, there seems to be a reluctance in the true nature of God to be visible, just as it is for the Holy Spirit to be present. There must be an element that causes them to be visible in the form of their creative visibility substance, and this substance is love that manifests itself within the humus temple (our bodies). It seems to make the Holy Spirit gain presence through the power of love to display itself as radiance in the humus body of God's creation. This is the immense light, a glow that radiates from the flesh. The scripture speaks of the radiance of the flesh in this fashion.

"The Son is the radiance of God's glory and the exact representation of his being, sustaining all things by his powerful word. After he had provided purification for sins, he sat down at the right hand of the Majesty in heaven" - Hebrews 1:3

In Ellicott's comments, he draws a more subjective view by his version of illumination of the light,

> *"Whom being the effulgence of His glory and the exact image of his substance. The first figure is familiar to us in*

the words of the Nicene Creed (themselves derived from this verse and a commentary upon it), "God of God, Light of Light, and Very God of Very God."

Again striking parallels to the language present themselves in Philo, who speaks of the spirit breathed into man at his creation as an "effulgence of the Blessed and Thrice-blessed Nature"; and in the well-known passage of the Book of Wisdom, "She (Wisdom) is the effulgence of the everlasting light, the unspotted mirror of the power of God, and the image of His goodness" (Wisdom Of Solomon 7:26).

In the Old Testament, the token of the divine presence is the Shechinah, the "cloud of glory" (called "the glory" in Romans 9:4; comp. Hebrews 9:5 in this Epistle); here it is the divine nature itself that is denoted by the "glory." Of the relation between this word and that which follows ("substance"), it is difficult to speak, as the conceptions necessarily transcend human language; but we may perhaps say (remembering that all such terms are but figurative) that the latter word is internal and the former external, --the latter the essence in itself, the former its manifestation. Thus the "Son" in His relation to "God" is represented here by light beaming forth from light, and by exact impress--the perfect image produced by stamp or seal."

The first key is this, ***"After HE had provided purification for sins" -Hebrew. 1:3 (NIV).*** In order for this light to be present in His creation, there had to be an eradication of sin before the light could be present. Jesus was sinless, so this light was present in Him, but the creatures who stood under God hadn't received regeneration in Christ (salvation).

Therefore, the light that was being placed before the creatures were revealed in Jesus but was denied by the creature based on a lack of knowledge. One example is in the book of Matthew,

"As soon as Jesus was baptized, he went up out of the water. At that moment, heaven was opened, and he saw the Spirit of God descending like a dove <u>and lighting on him</u>" - Matthew. 3:16 (NIV).

They received the invisibility of God based on their ability to understand the light that was mirrored in Jesus, which was mirrored in from God, who mirrored the same fleshly body as the Son, which we all received at the beginning of time.

When we recognize the light of Jesus, we see the visible nature of God, who is light. Again, as listed in the paragraph above,

"Again striking parallels to the language present themselves in Philo, who speaks of the spirit breathed into man at his creation as an "effulgence of the Blessed and Thrice-blessed Nature" and in the well-known passage of the Book of Wisdom, *"She (Wisdom) is the effulgence of the everlasting light, the unspotted mirror of the power of God, and the image of His goodness." Wisdom Of Solomon 7:26 , Charles J. Ellicott*

Let us use an example of how light works. *Ok, this isn't just about light but also how humans work. There are two ways that light could enter your eye. First, there could be a light source (like a light bulb) that creates light. This light then travels into your eye and BOOM - your brain interprets this signal as light. The other way (more common) is to see things by reflected light. Suppose you are looking at a pencil. The light (from somewhere) reflects off the pencil and then into your eye. But what happens if no light enters your eye? What if you are in a place with absolutely no source of light? In that case, you perceive* the color black. Actually, this can be a fun question. Ask someone this question:

Have you ever been somewhere with absolutely no light? (Most people haven't.)

If you were in a completely dark room, what would you see?

What happens after you wait a long, long time?

One very common answer is that you will see everything as black - at first. These humans will also say that, after some time, your eyes will adjust, and then you WILL see something. The correct answer is that you will just see black - forever. If there is no light entering your eyes, then you only see black. The common idea is based on a common experience. Normally, if you are in a dark room, your eyes DO indeed adjust. However, this only works in rooms with a little bit of light - and there is almost always at least a little bit of light." Allain Rhett

"This is the message we have heard from him and proclaim to you, that God is light, and in Him is no darkness at all" - 1John 1:5 (ESV)

> "Simply put, illumination in the spiritual sense is "turning on the light" of understanding in some areas. Throughout the ages, people in every culture and religion

have claimed some kind of revelation or enlightenment from God (whether true or not). When that enlightenment deals with new knowledge or future things, we call it prophecy. When that enlightenment deals with understanding and applying knowledge already given, we call it illumination. Regarding illumination of the latter type, the question arises, "How does God do it?"

Got Questions Ministries

This is a powerful analogy that references the light of God as it relates to Jesus being incarnated with the light of God. In the New Testament, the Apostle Paul seems to be saying that men cannot see God and live when he declares that God dwells in unapproachable light (1Tim. 6:16 NIV), but Jesus is filled with the light of God and is approachable. His source of light is contained by the flesh. God had placed himself in Jesus (The Son) as a buffer (fleshly body) when all who saw Jesus saw the source, which was God. This light of Christ traveled as a spiritual medium of illumination into their eyes and shed light into the dark caverns of their flesh. They were immediately illuminated by the light of God without "dying" but being allowed to approach Jesus (light of God) and receiving the image of God by the indwelling of the light of Christ.

In other words, they came from out of their darkness, the un-illuminated temples that their spirit dwelled in, seeing the reflective light of God in the body of Christ, as explained in Matthew 3:16. Although the multitudes didn't understand the illumination, even the disciples didn't see the light at first, they later understood, as Apostles, they had witnessed God in the flesh. This leads us to the understanding of the invisibility of God before us.

Chapter 6

The Invisibility of God Before Us

The protective covering of Yahweh is immanent in the Biblical references. Man wasn't truly aware of the Holy Spirit operating in Its invisible nature. However, God has placed in all creation the redemptive light, the invisibility of His general revelation that dwells in all creation, whether aware or unaware. Yahweh can decide to indwell through the Holy Spirit at any point in time and space through special revelation through observation, illusions, or the specific manifestation of that revelation. The below scripture pulls together the persuasive biblical passage relating to Yahweh's abilities to use general revelations invisibly through Yeshua that He had placed before His disciples to achieve special revelations through the Holy Spirit to speak the message of the good news gospel to those that he will bring forward to hear this message.

"But the Counselor, the Holy Spirit, whom the Father will send in my name, will teach you all things and will remind you of everything I have said to you" -John 14:26-28

"Jesus was speaking to His disciples in the upper room, giving them the last instructions before His resurrection. This special group of men was to be responsible for spreading the good news of Jesus Christ to the whole world. They had spent three and a half years with Him, watching His miracles and hearing His teachings.

They would relay those things to the rest of the world and would need God's special help remembering those things accurately. Jesus said the Holy Spirit would teach them and remind them of what had been said, so they could give it to others, which would include future revelations of the Gospels. This verse does not teach that the Spirit will do so with all believers. However, there are other verses that speak of the Spirit's illuminating work that will make corrections through man based on man's interpretations of what was written through Yeshua's teachings." Got Questions Ministries

"Therefore do not go on passing judgment before the time, but wait until the Lord comes who will both bring to light the things hidden in the darkness and disclose the motives of men's hearts; and then each man's praise will come to him from God" - 1 Corinthians 4:5 (NIV)

    The darkness of man's heart is the void of God's invisibility. What can be seen in darkness? Nothing but the desire to find a visible passage that can only be captured by the light. Man hides the truths given by the most High. This dark motive allows Yahweh's creation to become stagnant in cultural religions based on a system ruled by the antichrist of this time and his broken beliefs. Yes, we are eternal beings that never die, and Yahweh's breath is the truth and is everlasting.

Maveth is the Hebrew word for death or death personified. The Greek word for death is **Thanatos**, which is a mythology that means to die or dying.

Thanatos was a person, a minor figure that was often referred to as a person who rarely appeared. In this, Satan has built a realm of death that man must pass through in this life, all lies lead to death if we are not focused on the truths presented in the revelations given through the Holy Spirit; these truths that lay deeply embedded in scripture, which requires great investigation through study, when we don't investigate and study then, we look and sound like death, and practice a slow form of death. Yeshua defeated death by overcoming the realm of man and his defiled teachings, which were void of wisdom. Life in this realm has been defined by broken Kingdom interpretations of religious sects and their own worldview kingdom principles void of Yahweh's Holy Spirit.

"For from within, out of the heart of man, come evil thoughts, sexual immorality, theft, murder, adultery, coveting, wickedness, deceit, sensuality, envy, slander, pride, foolishness. All these evil things come from within, and they defile a person"
-Mark 7:21-23 (NIV)

In an article by Darius Stewart, *"The Darkness of Darkness,"* he illustrates the void of the invisibility of God in man. Take note that, when a man resists the incarnation of even the invisible nature of God inside himself and refuses acknowledgment of Yahweh, there is darkness:

"Amidst one of the darker days of Israel, we have this sad commentary: "For they are a nation void of counsel, neither is there any understanding in them. O that they were wise, that they understood this, that they would consider their latter end!" (Deut. 32:28). The "latter end" for the rich man is found in Luke 12:20: "But God said unto him, thou fool, this night thy shall be required of thee." This is not God's visible nature, but His invisibility speaking. "In Deuteronomy 32:28 are three things which describe the nation, yea, the individual: they are said to be void of counsel; to be void of

understanding; to be void of wisdom. And so it is with all mankind, whether they are Jew or Gentile: "they are all under sin. There is none that understands, there is none that seeketh after God" (Rom. 3:9b, 11. (Were it not for pure Grace, we would still be in that camp!)

"And the light shineth in the darkness; and the darkness comprehended it not" (John 1:5). They are void because they are in Darkness. May we further say that they are not only in the midst of, or surrounded by darkness, but are embedded in a cesspool of darkness? Moreover, I would contend that they might be rightly addressed as darkness. Darkness is a great void. It is mindless; it is incapable of any degree of comprehension."

In his article, Darius Stewart views darkness as without the substance of God; however, God is present even in the unregenerate man. Although darkness, in Stewart's mind, is a sign of wickedness, he also resounds the event of wisdom in the form of counsel towards the understanding, *"He cannot, He will not."* But those who believe are given over to the form of light to move from darkness to the futility of light away from the darkness of void. The void is lifted from darkness; the invisibility of God's recognition of light overcomes the void of darkness in the reflective light into the soul of the creative human to be enlightened.

"For ye were sometimes darkness, but now are ye light in the Lord: walk as children of the light" -Eph. 5:11 (NIV)

In an article presented by Antonio DeAgular, *"The Superior being known as God, Yahweh, The Lord,"* DeAgular writes of the invisible Yahweh, as seen in the image of Yeshua-Hamashiach, who is Jesus Christ the Messiah.

"John 5:37, "And the Father Himself, who sent Me [Jesus], has testified of Me. You have neither heard His [YHWH's] voice at any time, nor seen His [YHWH's] form."

John 11:4, "When Jesus heard that, He said, "This sickness is not unto death, but for the glory of God, that the Son of God may be glorified through it." (Healing of the sick)

John 11:40 "Jesus said to her, "Did I not say to you that if you would believe you would see the glory of God?"

John 14:7, "If you had known Me [Jesus], you would have known My Father [YHWH] also; and from now on, you know Him and have seen Him."

John 14:9, "Jesus said to him, "Have I been with you for so long, and yet you have not known Me, Philip? He who has seen Me has seen the Father; so how can you say, 'Show us the Father?'"

Romans 3:23, "For all have sinned and fall short of the glory of God,"

2 Corinthians 4:4, "Whose minds the god of this age [Satan] has blinded, who do not believe, lest the light of the gospel of the glory of Christ, who is the image of God, should shine on them."

2 Corinthians 4:6, "For it is the God who commanded the light to shine out of darkness, who has shone in our hearts to give the light of the knowledge of the glory of God in the face of Jesus Christ."

Colossians 1:15, "He [Jesus] is the image of the invisible God, the firstborn over all creation.

Hebrews 1:3, "[Jesus] who being the brightness of His [YHWH's] glory and the express image of His [YHWH'S] person, and upholding all things by the word of His power, when He had by Himself purged our sins, sat down at the right hand of the Majesty on high."

Can you see the Image of YHWH in the image (emphasis on image) of Jesus? He is a Good Shepherd, knew no sin to possess the glory of God, had compassion for all people, healed, fed and prayed for them, was an example of light to the world by teaching God's truth/way to eternal life and the Kingdom of God, laid down his life as an atonement for humanity, refuted falsehood by upholding and proclaiming Scripture/God's Word, outwitted his murderous opponents by his wisdom, and He Himself took our infirmities and bore our sicknesses. By His stripes, we are healed and found not guilty. This is why the name Yeshua was used to define Elohim. Yahweh inside of Yeshua.

Isaiah 53:4: "Behold! My Servant whom I have chosen, My Beloved in whom My soul is well pleased! I will put My Spirit upon Him, And He will declare justice to the Gentiles. He will not quarrel nor cry out, nor will anyone hear His voice in the streets. A bruised reed He will not break, and smoking flax He will not quench, Till He sends forth justice to victory; And in His name, Gentiles will trust."

Psalm 78:2: "I will open My mouth in parables; I will utter things kept secret from the foundation of the world." (Jesus using Parables)

Luke 4:18-21: "The Spirit of the Lord is upon Me Because He has anointed Me To preach the gospel to the poor; He has sent Me to heal the brokenhearted, To proclaim liberty to the captives And recovery of sight to the blind, to set at liberty those who are oppressed."

Isaiah 61:1,2: "To proclaim the acceptable year of the Lord."

Then He [Jesus] closed the book and gave it back to the attendant and sat down.

And the eyes of all who were in the synagogue were fixed on Him."

" And He [Jesus] began to say to them, "Today this Scripture is fulfilled in your hearing."

"However, although as the Infinite One, Yahweh, cannot be seen, not even by angelic spirit beings (once again, there is no form or shape to infinity) yet out of Himself, Yahweh's own Eternal Life has been eternally birthed, or emanated, as the perfect image or expression of Himself as He relates to His creation.

In other words, we can say that Yahweh, the Infinite Invisible Source of All Things, has Himself eternally come forth, shone forth, as an uncreated spirit being, in a form that is visible to His created spirit beings. It is the perfect Manifestation (the Perfect Living Image) of what Yahweh is as He relates to His universe of created spirit beings - angels, seraphim, cherubim, etc.

Yet, there is no separation between the Infinite One and that spirit being that is the continual outflowing, or birthing forth, of His own substance in a spirit form visible to others, created, spirit beings.

In Hebrew, this living manifestation of Yahweh is called Debar (called "Memra" by some), and in Greek, He is called the "Logos." Both terms in English mean "the Word" or "the Expression." Being that which Yahweh sends forth continuously of His own substance, the Dabar, or Word of Yahweh, is both Yahweh Himself (His own Eternal Life substance) and, at the same time, that which is with Him (as His Word, or Expression of Him). As the Eternal Life of Yahweh, this Expression of Yahweh has thus always existed with Yahweh.

John 1:1 expresses it this way, "In the beginning was the Word, and the Word was with Yahweh (or Elohim), and the Word was Yahweh (or Elohim)."

"The best illustration of this, that I know of is one from nature, which Yahweh Himself revealed to me when I sought Him for an answer to this mystery around 42 years ago. It is the sun, our solar system. Whatever the sun is, we know it by its glory or splendor that bursts

forth from it to our eyes (the image that it produces of itself by the light that it sends forth). And we know it by the warmth we experience from the energy that comes with and in the light.

So it is, that Yahweh, the Infinite One, is known by the glory, which He manifests of Himself (the living Word which in the course of time became Yeshua the Messiah). And we know Him by the totally invisible power of His life (the Holy Spirit), which operates in, through, and along with that glory."

"You cannot separate the sun, whatever that created mass in the sky is, from the light that shines out of it (and the energy power that comes in and with that light). Nor can you separate the light and power that is coming out of it from the sun that is the continual source of that outflowing light and power. The sun, whatever it is, is the continual supply of that which is its glory (its outshining light) and of its accompanying energy output. All three - the sun, it's light, and its energy -are distinguishable by definition and yet integrally, inseparable, one. Not one exists without the other existing.

So also, though in an infinitely greater way, Yahweh and His Word, which is His living image and glory (now made flesh in Yeshua), and His felt or experienced, invisible, but manifest, presence (the Holy Spirit) are distinguishable by definition, and yet are integrally, inseparably, One Elohim."

"*Thus, Yahweh exists not as two or three totally separate individuals, or personages, but as One Eternal Person or Being who is Themself Infinite. Yet They manifests Themself by the continuous out flowing of Themself, i.e., of His own Eternal Life, in a spirit form (Greek "morph" - Phil. 2:6), which is visible to other spirit beings as the "Word" or "Expression" of Yahweh.*

The Spirit is also manifested by a Presence of Power that is generally not seen at all but is experienced (by being felt, or by being expressed in acts of His power or might) as the Holy Spirit. Each, the Infinite, the Word, and the Spirit dwells integrally in the other even as the sun is in its rays and energy, and its rays and energy are in the sun."

"Therefore, outside Itself, They are always spoken of as being One, and only One. Thus, The Spirit and the holy prophets and apostles speak of Yahweh with singular pronouns. Yet within Yahweh is a complex, compound Being, who is triune in nature. Within Yahweh's triune nature, The Spirit can and does communicate within Itself, just as It would if It were three separate beings.

However, Yahweh is not three separate beings, but One Eternal, Infinite Being who exists simultaneously in three different modes. Yahweh is One Elohim, who manifests Itself by the living Word and by Its living Spirit. The confusion comes when people misunderstand the facts about the Spirit, Yahshua, the Messiah, who is the Word of Yahweh made flesh (John 1:14), and of whom Col. 2:9 speaks when it says, "For in Him dwells all the fullness of the Divinity bodily."

We have to use a clear understanding and careful analysis when we read John1: 14, which says, *"And the Word was made flesh"* and the related verses that tell of Yahshua's conception in the virgin womb of Miriam (Mary): Matt. 1:20 and Luke 1:31-35 (esp. 35). Since Yahshua, the Messiah is spoken of as having come down from heaven (John 6:51 and elsewhere), and since He is spoken of as the Eternal Life, which was with the Father and was made manifest unto us (I John 1:1,2), this question needs to be asked: *When the Glory, Expression, or Eternal Life of Yahweh ('the Word') became flesh, as a fetus in the womb of Miriam (and consequently as the newborn child Jesus of Nazareth), was all of Yahweh's Glory, all His Expression, all His Word, or all His Eternal Life contained only in the womb of Miriam (and, then, after birth, in the child that was born) in total quantity or just in total quality?*

I believe the answer must clearly be, *"In total quality, but not in total quantity."* Just as one drop of seawater is the same as the rest of the sea in quality but not in quantity, so it is that, when the Eternal Life or Word of Yahweh came down from heaven, we have no reason to suppose that the Eternal Life or Word of Yahweh did not still exist outside the man Yeshua the Messiah as well.

Though it is a great mystery as to how such a wonder took place, what clearly appears to have happened when the Holy Spirit - Yahweh in His non-seen but experienced form - overshadowed Miriam is that the Word, Yahweh's own Eternal Life, as it had been seen in heaven, in total quality but in tiny, minute quantity, was united to the seed or ova of a woman in place of the human sperm. This caused a conception, which was of Yahweh, so that the Holy Child thus born was the only begotten son of Yahweh, who then grew as time went by in understanding and stature like any other child would. He was thus the Son of Man (as He delighted to call Himself) and the Son of Yahweh (which He came to realize as He developed reasoning powers in early childhood). He was and is indeed the Word, the Eternal Life, now manifest in the flesh, as having been in this manner made flesh.

It might make this concept easier to understand if we remember that Levi was in the loins of Abraham long before he came to be born (Heb. 7:9-10). So also, the Eternal Life, or Word, was in Yahweh long before He came to be the man Yeshua the Messiah of Israel.

His historical birth or beginning as the man Jesus of Nazareth was when He was born in Bethlehem. He did not pre-exist as that except in the plan and purpose of Yahweh. But as the Word that (in the manner already described) became flesh, He existed with, and as, Yahweh from all eternity (John 1:1).

Thus, as He grew in understanding, He came to recognize,

1. He came from Yahweh and was one with Yahweh.

2. Yahweh (as the Infinite Being and as the non-bodily form by which the Infinite Being manifested Himself in the spirit realm) was His Father by means of Holy Spirit conception.

So, when people ask those who see this truth, such questions as, "Well, then, did Jesus pray to Himself?" the answer is "Absolutely not." The person Yeshua the Messiah did not as such pray to Himself. He, the man Jesus the Messiah, who was the Word made flesh, prayed to His Father Yahweh, who, although He was in the Son and the Son in Him (John 14:10,11), was at the same time still in heaven being seen by the angelic host (Matt. 18:10), while in His Infinity was, nevertheless, unable to be seen at all (John 1:18). Because He was Yahweh's Eternal Life made flesh, the man Yahshua could say, *"He that has seen me has seen the Father" (John 14:9), and could say, "My Father and I are one."* (John 10:30)

Yet, as being a man, Yeshua could also well say, *"My Father is greater than I."* Just as the spring of water is greater than the water that continually flows from it, even though the water that flows from it is the same substance, just as the sun is greater than the radiance and heat energy that comes out of it even though it is one with its rays and with their accompanying energy heat. Elohim (the Word and the Infinite Source of the Word), of which Jesus is the fleshly manifestation, was greater than the man, which He became by the incarnation in that miraculous virgin birth by the Holy Spirit. Because He was the total quality (though obviously not the total quantity) of Yahweh as His Expression and Life made flesh (now dwelling in, and limited to, the flesh as far as His humanity was concerned) He could pray, as He did pray, to be taken back and united, now in His humanity, to Yahweh by His being glorified with the glory that He had with the Father before the world began (John 17:5).

This is what took place when Yahshua was glorified after His resurrection. As the glorified man (now made a life-giving spirit according to I Cor. 15:45), Yahshua is both seated, visible to those in heaven, in His glorified body at the right hand of the Majesty on High that is next to Yahweh's non-bodily manifestation, yet is also come invisibly by the Holy Spirit to indwell His people, as Messiah in us (See John.14: 18-20). After all, enemies are put under His feet, in the execution of the victory of Calvary, then (in a way not now seen) the Son, the glorified man, Yahshua the Messiah will be subject to the Father so that Yahweh may be all in all.

As far as a submission is concerned, Yeshua is now and has always been submitted to the will of Yahweh in all things. So this must mean something different. When thinking about this many years ago, in my mind's eye, I saw a vision of a great marvelous light with the figure or silhouette of a man superimposed upon it as being the ultimate state of the man Yeshua the Messiah. On that day, the man Yahshua the Messiah will no longer be seen or appear to operate as separate from Yahweh but as fully one with Yahweh. As Revelation 22:3, 4 indicates, there will be one throne: *"the throne of Yahweh and the Lamb."* It says, *"His servants"* (the servants of "Yahweh and the Lamb") *"shall serve Him, and they shall see His face"* (the face of "Yahweh and the Lamb"), *"and His name"* (the name of "Yahweh and the Lamb) "shall be in their foreheads."* The antecedent of all these singular pronouns, "His," is *"Yahweh and the Lamb."*

I do not say we know the full answer for sure, but I am convinced this fully visible union of the man Yahshua the Messiah with the Eternal One (making Yahweh *"all in is all"*), is what's meant by the son being "subject unto" Yahweh. That is when we will fully see the revelation of Yahshua the

Messiah in the sense of which Rev. 22:3-4 and Zech. 14:9 speaks. We have seen the Bible plainly declare that Yahweh is One. He is never spoken of or speaks of Himself, in the plural. Only within His own being is He compound and complex. However, this is not as a plurality of persons or individuals but as having three simultaneous modes of existence or manifestations, each intertwined or dwelling in the other. He exists as the Infinite, Eternal, Unseen, and Unseeable One.

This is not the same as "dynamic modalism," which teaches God changed into the son and then back and forth into the Father and then the Spirit, etc., i.e., kept switching back and forth as one and then the other mode of manifestation. At the same time, He exists as the Manifestation of Himself, called the Word (or Expression) of Yahweh by which He is seen in the heavens and by which He has made appearances unto men (such as Abraham, Moses, Nadab, Abihu, and the 70 elders of Israel).

The Word is spoken of as being in the beginning with Yahweh, and yet as being Yahweh. He also exists as the totally invisible presence by which He manifests His omnipotence (His all-powerfulness). As such, He is felt and experienced by His creatures (e.g. Gen. 1:2 f, book of Acts, etc.). Thus, Yahweh is a complex, compound, triune being that communicates within Itself. It is to some extent like the sun, which sends forth a visible image -its radiance -, as well as an invisible, but experienced, or felt a presence from itself.

However, as an ever-living person, rather than a created substance as is the sun, that which Yahweh thus produces or sends forth out of Itself as Its manifestations, carries all the personality traits of Its person so that It can communicate within Itself. Yahweh can communicate among His own manifestations, sort of like we humans communicate with ourselves within our own individual beings. However, although there is a distinction made of Yahweh's existing manifestation (His simultaneous modes of existence), there is never a separation into three separate individuals or persons as we use that word "person" today.

This is why we read in John 1:1 that the Word is both with Yahweh and is Yahweh; nevertheless, we read that there is only One El, or Mighty One, as Isaiah 45:22 says as well as many other scriptures.

Finally, in order to redeem mankind by dying in his place and to bring mankind into His own glory, Yahweh, by The Word (or Eternal Life), became flesh. This Yahweh did by that Word being united to the ova or seed of woman by the Holy Spirit in minute quantity but in the fullness of quality. This virgin born child was the Son of Yahweh by being born of the Holy Spirit. [By Yahweh's Spirit the very living Word of Yahweh or the Eternal Life (in place of the human sperm) activated or gave life to the "seed of the woman" (the ova).] Thus, by virtue of His being born of the Holy Spirit, He "by inheritance obtained a more excellent name than" the angels (Heb.1: 4), who though they were called "the sons of Elohim," were created beings and not "the only begotten Son of Elohim," nor "the image of the invisible Elohim," nor "all the fullness of Elohim dwelling bodily," nor "the true Elohim and Eternal Life." The man Yahshua of Nazareth, the Messiah of Israel, by virtue of His birth by the Holy Spirit as "the Word" made flesh was all of this.

In other words, He was and is Elohim by inheritance as the Word of Elohim made flesh. Also, He is Elohim by virtue of the fact that, in his human spirit, He was given the Holy Spirit without measure. He had the infinite supply of the Holy Spirit. Yet being fully human, he had to learn obedience and overcome this world by constantly relying on the Father, Yahweh, and by prayer and the word, by walking in the spirit and not in flesh (even sinless flesh in His case). He had to walk by His human spirit to which the Holy Spirit was joined (in the infinite measure in His case, His being Elohim in the flesh) instead of obeying the natural desires created by the constant assault of the pressures of this world system of darkness as it worked upon His normal, natural sensibilities of the body. Though "Elohim" by grammatical construction is regarded as plural, it is sometimes used as a plural of intensity or majesty rather than number. Proof of this is that it is used of the false 'god' Chemosh (Judges 11:24), of the false "god" Dagon (I Samuel 5:7), and of Moses (Exodus 4:16). However, "El" as used in Isa. 45:22 and elsewhere of Yahweh is, by grammatical construction, only singular and is never used as a plural and natural mind through which the body works.

Unlike Adam, who obeyed a natural desire in disobedience to the word of Yahshua in His human form, will always choose to do the will of the Father, Yahweh, instead of the will of His natural, physical, fully normal, human desires for comfort, ease, pleasure, etc., even when the circumstances of this world played upon those desires drawing Him to satisfy them even at times when it was not in line with the Father's will. Thus, as a man walking according to His spirit, which was joined to the Holy Spirit, instead of walking according to His flesh or bodily desires, He overcame the kingdom of darkness.

We now, who have become born of Yahweh, also have the Holy Spirit joined to our spirit (though in limited, but as needed in increasing, measure). Therefore, we too, by this same Holy Spirit, who is now Messiah living in us, are able to get free from the flesh and to overcome the world, obeying the word of Yahweh by walking in spirit by the power of the same Holy Spirit of Yahweh.

As a final word, we read in I Timothy 3:16:

"And great is the mystery of the Deity; He who was manifest in the flesh, justified in spirit, seen of angels, preached unto the Gentiles, believed on in the world, received up into glory." Hallelujah!

As Yahweh's invisible nature is revealed as power and light, should HE be recognized as just that? As we ponder this question, we must reflect back to earlier statements about His qualities. Yahweh was not concerned about His appearance in any place in the bible nor the Torah, so why should we be concerned? It is our nature to be inquisitive. We are people of substance, and we desire substance. Our very essence is of the material substance; we judge people based on their appearance, just as Israel based their deity on appearance. If Yahweh is light, should we worship the light, or should we worship in spirit? Yahshua was of the flesh, and many people worship His fleshly appearance from the biblical references. We see Jesus as an object and words; we can't fathom nor justify the true spiritual attributes of EL because of our fleshly desires that dismiss the fact that Yahweh is Holy and not born, but to us, he is emphatical of this world.

In our own forceful measures, without doubt, we dismiss the invisible nature of Yahweh and choose a language (anthropomorphisms) to describe His particular being as a significant being, a striking emphatic power that relates to our worldview. We, who have become born of Yahweh, also have the Holy Spirit joined to our spirit (though in limited, but as needed in increasing, measure). Therefore, we too, by this same Holy Spirit, who is now the Messiah living in us through breath, are able to get free from the flesh and are enabled to overcome the world, by obeying the word of Yahweh, and by walking in the spirit by the power of the same Holy Spirit of Yahweh.

The bold extremities of a tyrannical systematic theocracy that hold us hostage in a medley of philosophical, psychological entrapments that compel us to visualize the truths of the invisible nature of Yahweh become mythical nonsense to an alarming percentage of humans. In such a system as today, doesn't it resemble the systems of Pharaoh and the Greek and the Roman Empire? Suppression rules the flesh and entraps the spirit; the point that is being made is that we're repeating history on a higher platform with technology as the master.

The true nature of the Holy Spirit is being suppressed in the body and can't be expressed; frequencies form a barrier around our humus bodies (radio, television, cell phones, and microwaves). These barriers weaken our perception by weakening our flesh, which allows our spirits to be exposed to the personification of evil as it conceived in many and various cultures and religious traditions.

It is seen as the objectification of a hostile and destructive force. Take Pharaoh as an example. He knew, if he kept the Hebrews under constant surveillance through fear, placing rations on food and water, under extreme working conditions, by design, this would take the Hebrews' minds away from the invisible spirited initiative given by Yahweh to praise; this was the spiritual gumption of Satan to put away the thoughts of being slaves and praising Yahweh; he deterred them by manipulating the flesh. Pharaoh was reacting just as the prince of the kingdom of Persia did (Satan), masking a spirit of suppression that masked itself as starvation in the midst of the Hebrews; hunger and thirst blocked their ability to praise Yahweh. Their praises weren't coming before God, but God knew that even hunger was temporary because, if the multitudes perished, there would be no slaves to do the work, but Pharaoh's heart was hardened past the population of slaves. He wanted them to be fearful of him.

The same scenario applies in modern history; if Satan blocks the invisibility of God that stands before us through fear, suffering, starvation, then praises to God will be temporarily withstood, but God will breakthrough. He uses the humus body that houses His Spirit to achieve the impossible. What is impossible for man is made possible by Yahweh. Yahweh will turn it around.

Chapter 7

Sanctification by Authority

Today, the raising of a new spirit called "Nationalism" is challenging the Spirit Yahweh. This nationalism schism is calling for Evangelical Christians to sew their roots into the fabric of America as a form of religion. This form of religion breaks the invisible nature of Yahweh in the believer. It turns their desire towards another inferior god that challenges the true nature of the Holy Spirit that was given to all creation. Nationalism doesn't define us; the Holy Spirit that Yahshua placed before us defines us and strengthens the body, mind, and soul.

Sanctification is Yahweh's Will for us. This sanctification is rooted in the word saint; both words are related to holiness. Sanctifying something or someone is to set it apart for a specific use; to sanctify a person is to make that person Holy.

Sanctification brings us in to view the reality that we have been set aside from the worldly ways of man's secular schisms and placed within the realm of justification, maturity, and glorification. In this article, the writer has bestowed upon the believer what the Bible speaks about our sanctified temples being placed into the invisible salvation in Yeshua.

Jesus had a lot to say about sanctification in John 17. In verse 16 the Lord says, *"They are not of the world, even as I am not of it,"* and this is before His request: *"Sanctify them by the truth; your word is truth"* (verse 17).

In Christian theology, sanctification is a state of separation unto God; all believers enter into this state when they are born of God: *"You are in Christ Jesus, who came to us wisdom from God, righteousness and sanctification and redemption"* (1 Corinthians 1:30, ESV). The sanctification mentioned in this verse is a once-for-ever separation of believers unto God. It is a work God performs, an intricate part of our salvation, and our connection with Christ (Hebrews 10:10). Theologians sometimes refer to this state of holiness before God as "positional" sanctification; it is the same as justification.

While we are positional holy ("set free from every sin" by the blood of Christ, Acts 13:39), we know that we still sin" (1 John 1:10).

That is why the Bible also refers to sanctification as practical experience of our separation unto God. "Progressive" or "experiential" sanctification, as it is sometimes called, is the effect of obedience to the Word of God in one's life. It is the same as growing in the Lord (2 Peter 3:18) or spiritual maturity. God started the work of making us like Christ, and He is continuing it (Philippians 1:6). This type of sanctification is to be pursued by the believer earnestly (1 Peter 1:15; Hebrews 12:14) and is effected by the application of the Word (John 17:17).

> *"Progressive sanctification has in view the setting apart of believers for the purpose for which they are sent into the world: "As you sent me into the world, I have sent them into the world. For them, I sanctify myself, that they too may be truly sanctified" (John 17:18–19). That Jesus set Himself apart for God's purpose is both the basis and the condition of our being set apart (see John 10:36).*
>
> *We are sanctified and sent because Jesus was. Our Lord's sanctification is the pattern of and power for our own. The sending and the sanctifying are inseparable. On this account, we are called "saints" (hagioi in the Greek), or "sanctified ones." Prior to salvation, our behavior bore witness to our standing in the world in separation from God, but now our behavior should bear witness to our standing before God in separation from the world. Little*

by little, every day, "those who are being sanctified" (Hebrews 10:14, ESV) are becoming more like Christ.

There is a third sense in which the word sanctification is used in Scripture—a "complete" or "ultimate" sanctification. This is the same as glorification. Paul prays in 1 Thessalonians 5:23, May the God of peace himself sanctify you completely, and may your whole spirit and soul and body be kept blameless at the coming of our Lord Jesus Christ" (ESV).

Paul speaks of Christ as "the hope of glory" (Colossians 1:27) and links the glorious appearance of Christ to our personal glorification: "When Christ, who is your life, appears, then you also will appear with him in glory" (Colossians 3:4). This glorified state will be our ultimate separation from sin, total sanctification in every regard.

We know that when Christ appears, we shall be like him, for we shall see him as he is" (1 John 3:2). "To summarize, "sanctification" is a translation of the Greek word hagiasmos, meaning "holiness ` or "a separation." In the past, God granted us justification, a once-for-all, positional holiness in

Christ. Now, God guides us to maturity, a practical, progressive holiness. In the future, God will give us glorification, permanent, ultimate holiness. These three phases of sanctification separate the believer from the penalty of sin (justification), the power of sin (maturity), and the presence of sin (glorification)." Gotquestion.org

In the book of Genesis chapter 1:26-27 (NIV), **"Then God said, Let us make man in our own image," this is justification, "in our likeness," this is equal to maturity, "and let them rule over the fish of the sea and the birds of the air, over the livestock, and over the earth, and over the creatures that move along the ground."**

God glorified the creatures and gave them dominion. This is the invisibility of God in us, *"God created man in His own image, and in the image of God, he created him; male and female he created them."* In Genesis Chapter 5:2, royalty was given to man and woman when God said, *"He created them male and female and blessed them."* Whenever God speaks and makes a proclamation, it becomes law, and God's laws can never be broken!

When we understand the invisible nature of God, only then can we understand the authority He has manifested in us; that authority was given by God, which makes it law! God is a Spirit. He will not interfere in the realm of His creation. It will only be done in Spirit;

therefore, Yahweh needed a dirt body to come into this realm to speak in the flesh to creation. That is why we are so important. We have a body with a Spirit, and God needs us so that HE can direct us towards what HE has planned for us to do, even while we were still in HIM; we were created to transcend time while in these dirt bodies; Jesus did it.

Dr. Myles Monroe of the Bahamas, who is a mighty "Man of God," figured out what this invisibility of God was all about. I will quote but paraphrase Dr. Monroe,

"On earth, man can't do anything without God and vice versa. God will do nothing on earth without man. We have a partnership with God and a partnership with heaven and earth. It is important that we know the power of prayer. Prayer is an earthly license for heavenly interference. Prayer isn't an option; it is a necessity for believers. With this, the power of the human is of most importance, we learn that we don't have a spirit, but we are a spirit!"

This is the importance of the invisibility of Yahweh; we are HIS Invisible Spiritual agents in a dirt body here on earth; we were brought here as Yahweh's Glory to inhabit His visible earthly Kingdom, to figure out what the invisible Kingdom of heaven looks like on a visible planet called earth. Our dirt bodies are proof that we're temporarily here to seek the truths of Yahweh through Yeshua.

"Yeshua told the woman at the well that Yahweh was spirit and did not dwell in mountains, rivers, trees, and was not confined to one place. He is spirit whereby He permeates the earth and the universe. Yahweh is a Spirit: and they that worship Him must worship him in spirit and in truth" - **John 4:24**

CHAPTER 8

LOOKING BEYOND

In this chapter, the passages quoted are thoughts about where we are in this realm or physical plane and the realm above us. It is explored as a measure of our ability to transform our realities into the teachings of the Apostle Paul's words and visions. Paul spoke in 2 Corinthians 12:2 about a vision from the third heaven (which is covered later in this book, relating to Dionysius the Areopagite, which deals with the Dominations, Virtues, and the Powers) that gave Paul wisdom beyond the understanding of men of his time. This nature that Paul received is the blurred lines between our realities, and that in which God has stored for those who see and trust His invisibility to be present in the earthly realm. This is the gift of the Holy Spirit that desires to engage with our internal spirit given by God.

Remember, our flesh is contaminated by this world and is separated from the visible Kingdom of Yahweh that is in our midst. The Holy Spirit desires to be one in spirit with Yahweh's creation; however, we must relinquish this ineffective deity, so that the Holy Spirit will once again become one with the spirit of Yahweh's creative beings.

In an article posted online by Yahweh's Assembly in Yeshua (unknown author), the writer of this article states:

"It is beyond the physical, in the unseen, invisible realm where Yahweh abides. The spirit realm is a step above the physical. Man cannot go beyond the edge of our physical realm because he is held back by human limitations. Although the spirit realm is a step beyond our physical boundary, we can in a measure gain perceptions of the spirit realm, but "through a glass, darkly, which means to have an obscure or imperfect vision of reality; the Apostle Paul explains that "we do not now see clearly, but at the end of time, we will do so."

Regarding these two realms, which Yeshua could move, the first is the physical realm. He also had access to the second, which is the spiritual realm. The first is visible; the second is invisible. We are quite familiar with our normal physical realm here on earth. Matter occupies space and is something we can see, touch, weight, feel, or prove exists. The physical plane is where mankind resides. There is also the spirit realm, which is also very real. This is where Yahweh, Yeshua, and celestial beings abide and move. Just as man is limited in physical aspects, in comparison to Yahweh, he is even more limited in the spirit realm. Yahweh's concepts or thoughts surpass those of man:

"For My thoughts are not your thoughts, nor your ways My ways, says Yahweh. For as the heavens are higher than the earth, so are My ways higher than your ways, and My thoughts than your thoughts." -Isaiah 55:8-9 (MKJV)

Following Yeshua's baptism, it was said, *"lo the heavens were opened unto Him."* **(Matthew 3: 16).** The Holy Spirit descended upon Him, giving Yahshua free access to the spiritual realm. We have also given the earnest of the Holy Spirit when we are baptized into His name (Acts 2:38). Yahweh's Holy Spirit was given in its fullness to the Savior. Yeshua's thoughts and ways then reached beyond the physical realm and were higher than mankind's thoughts. We are given examples that show Yahshua moving in the spirit realm, which permeates the physical. He often perceived even the thoughts of His disciples:

"And Yahshua knew their thoughts, and said unto them, every kingdom divided against itself is brought to desolation, and every city or house divided against itself shall not stand."-**Matthew 12:25 (AV).**

(Note: This serves as an example to the USA, we are greatly divided!)

"And Yeshua knowing their thoughts said, wherefore think ye evil in your hearts?
 -**Matthew 9:4 (AV)**

"And immediately when Yeshua perceived in his spirit that they so reasoned within themselves, he said unto them, why reason ye these things in your hearts?"
-**Mark 2:8 (AV) (Also, Psalms 139:2; John 21:17; 1 Corinthians 2: 11)**

We often hear of accounts from loved ones who were awakened from a sound sleep. Though separated by miles, they are suddenly aware that a husband, wife, relative or friend is in danger. Only later did they learn more fully of this phenomenon that occurred at the precise time, which is often unexplained. There is a realm that transcends our physical senses. Communication in the spirit realm will not depend upon the spoken word, but the thoughts will be perceived. Yeshua said, *"**The wind bloweth where it listeth, and thou hearest the sound thereof, but canst not tell whence it comes and whither it goes: so is every one that is born of the Spirit.**"- John 3:8*

When we are born of the spirit in the first resurrection, our bodies will be changed to pure energy. We will be invisible, no longer physical (unless we want to slow down our spirit bodies and become physical). We are aware of unseen physical powers, energy, or force, just as we are aware of the higher realm of the spirit.

- One can see the results of what wind does, even though we cannot see the wind.

- Neither can we see electricity, but we are aware of its potential.
- Gravity is a force we deal with every day, but we cannot see the power that pulls objects toward the center of this earth.

It is possible to have a number of forces active in your room right now. There could be gravity, radio waves, electricity, magnetism, subliminal sound waves, etc. One could turn on a flashlight and add another force or power that might not be noticed in daylight. Much like the unseen powers of the physical realm, this unseen world, known as the spirit realm, is invisible to the human eye. It reaches beyond our physical realm, and we are not always fully aware of it. It is in this spirit realm where our Heavenly Father, Yahweh, exists. Yeshua revealed to us. We cross into the spirit realm when we offer up prayers to Him and meditate on His power and existence.

Yahweh dwells in the spirit realm outside of time, matter, and space. He views the physical universe from His vantage of seeing the end from the beginning. He can look at an oak tree and see an acorn bursting out of its shell, groping for light. He can see it as a sapling, struggling to reach higher. He can see the oak tree as it is now and when it ages and decays. He lives in eternity, where time does not exist.

Yahweh has never crossed into the physical realm to be seen of men. He is King of kings and Lord of lords:

"Who only has immortality, dwelling in the light which no man can approach unto; Whom no man has seen, nor can see; to Whom be honor and power. So be it." - 1 Timothy 6:16

He abides in the spirit realm but has made provision for us eventually to rise up to Him through His Son, Yeshua. No one has seen the Heavenly Father at any time, for it was the Malach or the Angel of Yahweh that was active as Yahweh in the Old Testament.

Our Heavenly Father is invisible, a Spiritual being, eternal, immortal, and dwells in the spirit realm as a bright unapproachable light consisting of spiritual energy. Yahweh exists in the spirit realm where time does not exist, for time and space cannot abide where there isn't any matter. Yahweh has never left the spirit realm, yet He allowed Yeshua to come upon the earth to reveal the Heavenly Father. Yeshua is the only one we know of who has seen the Father and who has now joined Him in the heavenly realm:

"Now unto the King eternal, immortal, invisible, the only wise Elohim be honor and glory forever and ever. So be it."
- 1 Timothy 1:17 (AV)

Those who overcome in this age will have full access to Yahweh's invisible Spirit realm. This Spirit Realm could be right here among us. Being composed of Spirit energy, this realm is invisible to us, just as we now likely have radio waves, TV signals, and other energy types flowing through our homes and buildings, which we are not aware of unless we are tuned in with a receiver, such as a radio or television set.

- The spirit realm is hidden and ignored by most people and not understood by the great majority.
- The spirit realm is energy, force, power, and vitality, supernatural--above the physical. Remember, Satan's power of persuasion is also active in the spirit realm.

We are each a soul, spirit, and body. A brief study of the Biblical differences between soul and spirit reveals the soul is best understood as life itself. "Soul" is **nephesh** in Hebrew and **psuche** in Greek. We often read of a ship or airplane going down, and a certain number of "souls" were lost. Often, the word soul is used for the individual, as in "The soul that sinneth, it shall die" (Ezekiel 18:4, 18:20, also James 5:20). When the soul departs, life leaves the body. Without life, the body is dead.

The spirit (**ruach** in the Old Testament Hebrew, **pneuma** in the Greek of the New) is often best understood as wind or breath. The broader meaning of spirit is an unseen or invisible force or power. Spirit in Romans chapter eight clearly reveals a difference between the Holy Spirit from Yahweh, which is supernal, by which His acts are carried out. Although not found in the Bible, the Hebrew **SHEKINAH** is His bright, shining glory, His Holy Spirit.

It is by Spirit that He governs and rules and has power over creation. Yahweh's Spirit is the most powerful of all unseen forces at work in our environment. This Spirit overcomes all other forces in the world. It allows Yahweh to use other forces or energy to accomplish His will. Examples of the Shekinah glory was during Succoth when the Hebrews left Egypt, the cloud of glory that protected them from the intense sunlight of the day, and the pillar cloud of fire that provided light during the night to put distance between them and their enemies as they traveled to worship Yahweh in the desert.

Conversely, the spirit of man is carnal, worldly, and self-serving. The New Testament reveals our spirit is very much our attitude or mindset and what we think most of the time. Through baptism, we are given a portion of the Holy Spirit. We are to allow His Spirit to have full reign in all we do. We are to overcome our carnal spirit and allow Yahweh's Spirit to guide and dominate our lives so that we think and see things from the same perspective as Yahweh and Yeshua. Upon death, the spirit of man (breath of life) is given back to Yahweh. If we are in that first resurrection, we will be given the Holy Spirit in its fullness, as was Yeshua.

The body is governed by our mind or spirit. This we can understand, for it is physical and very real. When Yahweh created Adam, He molded him from the earth. He was brought to life only when Yahweh blew air (***Ruach***, the breath of life) into his nostrils, and he began to breathe:

"Then Yahweh Elohim formed a man of dust from the ground, and breathed into his nostrils the breath of life, and man became a living being [soul]." -Genesis 2:7 (RSV)

The book of Numbers carries the account of the prophet Balaam, who was so intent upon gaining a reward that the donkey upon which he was riding perceived the spiritual presence of the Angel of Yahweh blocking the path. However, Balaam was oblivious of the Angel, so intent was he on seeking his reward from the pagan king Balak. Finally, Yahweh opened Balaam's eyes to the spirit realm (Numbers 22:31). Seeing the Angel with a drawn sword, Balaam fell on his face. The donkey was aware of the Angel three times, but greedy Balaam's thoughts and attention were concentrated upon an expected reward. Concentration on worldly pursuits blinded his spiritual ability to perceive the angelic being.

Elisha, Yahweh's prophet, was able to discern what Israel's enemy, the king of Syria, discussed in his bedchamber (2 Kings 6:12-17). The king planned to take Elisha captive. When the young king, upon seeing all the enemies' horses and chariots encompassing the city, became frightened, Elisha reassured him, *"Fear not: for they that be with us are more than they that be with them."* (verse 16). In answer to Elisha's prayer, Yahweh opened the eyes of the young man so he could see the spirit realm, *"and behold, the mountain was full of horses and chariots of fire round about Elisha."* (verse 17).

Paul encourages us to be alert to the spiritual temptations and trials of the devil because he operates in the spirit realm. Our battles are far more spiritual than physical:

"Put on the whole armor of Yahweh so that you may be able to stand against the wiles of the devil. For we do not wrestle against flesh and blood, but against principalities, against powers, against the world's rulers, of the darkness of this age, against spiritual wickedness in high places." **Ephesians 6:11-12 (MKJV)**

It is clear that the spirit realm could well be among us right now, but we are unable to see it, touch it, taste it, or hear it. It is beyond our physical reach and comprehension.

"As That they should seek Yahweh, if haply they might feel after him, and find him, though he be not far from every one of us: For in Him we live, and move, and have our being." - **Acts 17:27-28 (ASV).**

All the above is to show that the spirit realm is not in some far-off galaxy somewhere. It is right here. Yahweh, the Father has never made Himself visible to human eyes. He has remained in the spirit realm, where He can watch His creation and keep tabs on everything that goes on in both our physical world and the spiritual realm. He cannot stand sin of any kind.

As a result, He has made a way through His Son, in which mankind can cleanse himself of sin and overcome his carnal nature. Therefore, He being made a spirit to join the great multitude that will be in the first resurrection, the Kingdom of Yahweh is within our grasp if we turn to Yahweh with a determined heart to be in that Kingdom. Yeshua went on to say:

"Verily, verily, I say unto thee, except a man be born again (born anew or from above) he cannot see the kingdom of Yahweh." -John 3:3 (ASV)

This will also be the goal of those who are seeking immortality and the promise of eternal life. The Elect and the great multitude, which make up that first resurrection, will become Yahweh's spiritual children. This means we must be changed to spirit beings, which is the promise to those who will be in that first resurrection, born into the spirit realm. This should be the goal of everyone:

"Blessed and holy is he that hath part in the first resurrection: on such the second death hath no power, but they shall be priests of Yahweh and of Messiah, and shall reign with Him a thousand years." -Revelation 20:6

"Now this I say, brethren, that flesh and blood cannot inherit the kingdom of Yahweh; neither doth corruption inherits incorruption." - 1 Cor. 15:50

Paul goes on to reveal that those in the first resurrection, whether dead or alive, will be made spirit beings. Those in the first resurrection will be made immortal and can die no more:

"Behold, I show you a mystery; we shall not all sleep, but we shall all be changed,

In a moment, in the twinkling of an eye, at the last trump: for the trumpet shall sound, and the dead shall be raised incorruptible, and we shall be changed.

For this, corruptible must put on incorruption, and this mortal must put on immortality.

So when this corruptible shall have put on incorruption, and this mortal shall have put on immortality, then shall be brought to pass the saying that is written, Death is swallowed up in victory." **-1 Corinthians 15:51-54 (AV)**

"They shall be like Him, for they shall see Him as He is, face to face." - 1 John 3:2.

If we are in that first resurrection, we will be joint-heirs of all things with Yeshua, sharing that same glorious light Yeshua now has with the Father. Now that the Holy Spirit has come to earth on the day of Pentecost in Acts 2, it is here to stay.

"Beloved, now are we the sons of Elohim, and it doth not yet appear what we shall be: but we know that, when he shall

appear, we shall be like him; for we shall see him as he is."-1 John 3:2 (AV)

In the above connotation, heaven is explained as a spiritual exaltation that is exhibited based on the spirit being exited from the body; however, another notation should be added as it relates to the invisibility of this same spirit being made available in the creature. In this, the creature (man) would see the promised land through the understanding of the obedience within the confines of the invisible spirit of Yahweh, while concentrating on worldly pursuits. This blinds the creature's spiritual ability to perceive the angelic realm.

We see the words in scripture, but our carnal nature blurs our perceptions to receive the vivid adaptations in its glorious nature. We're encouraged to be alert to the spiritual temptations and trials of Satan because he operates in the spirit realm. Because he is a fallen angel and understands God far better than humans, we must remember that an advocate has been given to us upon the earth that stands before us as the invisible nature of God in Christ, which communicates in prayer and supplication based upon the creature's ability to invite this Holy Spirit to come upon themselves.

Our battles are far more spiritual than physical and require our hidden attributes to acknowledge the Holy Spirit. We must be vested in its ability to be summoned at a moment's notice; it's done by the permission of God's creatures (Humans).

"Those whom I love I rebuke and discipline. So be earnest and repent. Here I AM!

I stand at the door and knock. If anyone hears my voice and opens the door, I will come in and eat with him, and He with me." -Rev. 3:19-20 (NIV)

The invisible spirit is calming in nature. Our site has been directed towards the spirit to see its invisibility. We do have the ability to see and interact with truth, and Yahweh has given such a gift to those who seek His truths, which are the keys to the Kingdom of Yahweh. As we move forward in this understanding, we will learn about the light that is present in this realm; based on what Yahweh has enacted in us is based on who and what He is, and this gift is the invisible nature of light as the spirit that indwells HIS creation.

CHAPTER 9
THE GIFT OF THE LIGHT (LIGHT TREASURES)

The Bible's explanation of Jesus calling the disciples was a twofold story about God inside a human that changed the heart of men and women forever. This story leads the readers on an adventure of the calling of twelve working-class men who have no idea what they are being led to do in the unfolding story of God inside Jesus while HE journeyed. The disciples just stopped in the middle of their careers and followed a stranger they'd never met; they knew nothing of the Messiah that stood before them.

The question that arises is, what did they see, hear, feel, or sense about this stranger that they had never encountered? What the Bible presents as a journey into patience, perils, deception, and a lesson of faith into the unknown presses even deeper into the true reason this spiritual man named Jesus would show up in the midst of these ordinary men and women to take them on a pathway towards the light of the Kingdom of Yahweh.

"Upper Galilee, where so many foreigners live, there are people who sat in darkness have seen a great light; they sat in the land of death, and the Light broke through upon them." -**Matthew 4:16 (TLB)**

Yeshua is a teacher to the disciples and all who witnessed the light treasure inside; the lesson that was being taught would far surpass what the Bible's printed words revealed. Yeshua is the light bearer of the world, the entire planet. The spiritual realm was within in HIS grasp, and all Yeshua wanted to do was show all creation The Father's way to the enlightened Kingdom that is present here on earth, but first HE had to show the disciples proof that the Kingdom of God was before them, that it existed in them as the Light Treasures that had been hidden from all creation. This is the primary reason that God continued to transcend time as the Holy Ghost so that the vessels that were interrupted at the beginning with Adam's fall could now be fulfilled and reconciled through Yeshua's teachings.

The Heavenly Kingdom is explained as being the invisible Word of Yahweh. Although invisible, the world knew of the spirit that resonated in the temples of their bodies but couldn't comprehend the intentions or the interactions within, they needed guidance. They who knew this had become children of the true Mind bringing down the invisible Kingdom of Heaven to a visible Kingdom called earth; they would witness the light of Yeshua. John the Baptist was one of these kingdom dwellers on earth.

The raising of Earth to Heaven is the ceasing from being an earthly intelligence by receiving the Word of the Gnosis and becoming a Dweller in Heaven on earth, which isn't impossible. The word Gnosticism is considered the principal element of salvation to be direct knowledge of the supreme divinity, experienced as intuitive or esoteric insight. Gnostic cosmogony presents a distinction between a supreme, transcendent God and a blind, evil demiurge responsible for creating the material universe, thereby trapping the divine spark within a matter of encrusted body; in other words, our spirit of breath being placed in a dirt body. This is why we're called a humus man-human temple.

The word humus is a word derived from the late 18th century from the Latin word that means soil. Man is a plural word that represents both man and woman, thus giving us the word human. We were created from dirt, formed in God's image, character, and integrity. The breath, the spark, this light is housed in our bodies, which means we are responsible as guardians of our bodies.

Those who focus on the light will receive its treasures, and they will be saved from the evil rulers of this world, Satan's imps, and he will become the midst (that is to say, perhaps, that they will be above the ruler of this world and no longer subject to him as a slave of fleshly matter; the ruler of the earthly kingdoms will be a "nothing" to them; that is to say, evil will have no effect on them that are of the light). The evil powers will envy the children of light because they know the light inside Jesus that is reflective in them, that He is not of this world, and that no evil comes from Him. But as for those who are born in the flesh of unrighteousness (and are not children of the Righteous Race, but those of the second birth, the spiritual rebirth), they have no part in the severed Kingdom of Heaven here on earth. Jesus said unto them,

"Verily, verily, I saw unto thee, except a man be born again, he cannot see the Kingdom of God." -John 3:3

The disciples were in despair because they became aware that they had been born of a broken system according to what they had been taught in error about their sinful nature in their fleshly bodies by the Jewish Pharisees, the teachers of the law, and this form of faith they had been born into. They were ruled by the colonization of a foreign power (Greco Roman Empire). Yeshua was amongst them and taught them that it was not the flesh of their bodies, but the unrighteousness and ignorance of what they had been exposed to that deterred them from receiving the truth. They were being taught in error to receive a broken form of religion. Their human temples had been placed in a placebo syndrome created by an evil man, a dictator.

In this understanding, the disciples were being awakened. They were asking to be instructed in the nature of ignorance, so they could understand the truth of the law from the Word (Jesus). Yeshua would teach them to understand the great mysteries of this realm based on what HIS FATHER taught inside HIS Temple. In order to understand the mysteries, they would first have to remove their cultural teachings and place themselves in purity as virgins in HIS truths and righteousness. They must put on the cloth of glory and seek to understand the teaching of the Word of Yahweh. In this way, the disciples would learn to know the truth and its fullness given through the Master. These disciples desired to learn and ask Yeshua, Thou Living One, to teach them the fullness that should indwell them, that they may be in the realm of truth and righteousness according to His words, and as they learned this message about the light treasures, their wisdom had exalted them towards the glorification of Apostles.

We, as seekers of the truth, have been placed in a whirlwind of propaganda. The Jewish and Greco Roman institutions have constructed and reconstructed these writings over and over for the past two centuries to fit their own nomenclature. While we seek the truth, we must look deeply into our souls to understand better the truths that are inscribed and embedded in our hearts and minds. This is the desire Yeshua continually has of HIS remnant,

"But seek ye first the Kingdom of God and its righteousness; and all these things will be added unto you." -Matt. 6:33 (KJV)

The New Testament had yet to be written, and a true teacher such as the Messiah hadn't instructed the Jews and gentiles in truth. Jesus instructed them,

"Don't misunderstand why I have come, it isn't to cancel the laws of Moses and the warnings of the prophets. No, I have come to fulfill them, and make them all come true." - Matthew 5:17 (TLB)

There is writing called " Schmidt's *Second Book of Ieou*," where we are introduced to the following narrative: "The Mysteries of the Treasure of Light." Jesus bids the twelve disciples, and the women disciples surround Him and promise to reveal to them the great mysteries of the Treasure of Light, which no one born of the Invisible God knows (that is to say, no one, even of the powers of the church that surrounds or is beyond or within the regions that surround them, understands the light treasures of the Invisible God as a ruler). If these mysteries are consummated, neither the rulers of synagogues nor those who were coming to learn of the Invisible God can endure the teaching of the Messiah nor comprehend them, for they are the great mysteries of the interiors of the Treasure of Light. When these are consummated, the Receivers of the Light-treasure come into a fuller understanding and bear the truths taught through all inferior spaces of this life into the Light-treasure that exists within their bodily temples. Yea, the sins of that soul, whether conscious or unconscious, are blotted out, and the soul becomes pure Light. And not only does the purified soul pass through all inferior spaces, but also within into the light-realm, ever inward, within all its spaces, orders, and powers, to the space of the Uncontainable in the innermost space of the Light-treasure. This is what Jesus was preparing the disciples for. This wasn't an adventure; they were being prepared for a journey into the body of Yeshua, so they could witness what HE saw through the light in which His Father had placed inside the flesh, which was the Messiah, the invisible nature of Yahweh.

As a witness, I can attest to this passage. When I was about 22 years old, I had a dental procedure done. I was put to sleep with laughing gas, as it is called. While asleep, I felt my spirit becoming more vibrant, resonant to the point that, suddenly, all I could see was light all about myself. There was a pronounced voice that spoke to me as I was spiraling, funneling forward. Upon the walls of this funneling effect were pictures of all the history of the world. It was so vivid. I saw pictures that I knew were true from the history I was taught through education, and there were pictures that I knew nothing about. They were pictures of future events to come. And then the pronounced voice sounded out with authority and said, "ALL LIES, ALL LIES, ALL LIES!" At that point, I was brought back to consciousness. I looked over to the sidewall of the room adjacent to the dental chair that I was sitting in, and the Doctor and his assistant both were crying profusely. I asked them in a weak voice, "Why are you guys crying?" and they turned to me, and both nearly jumped out of their skin and replied, "We had lost your pulse. We tried to resuscitate you but failed. We were trying to collect our emotions before we called the ambulance." I could fill the deepness of their relief.

These mysteries are to be guarded with secrecy and revealed to the few who are worthy, and to them alone. This light exists in Yahweh's creation, whether taught or denied. "Those alone are worthy of the mysteries of the Light-treasure (the emanation of the Unapproachable God), have centered their whole faith in the Light, giving ear to one another, and submitting themselves the one to the other, as do the children of the Light."

We alone have been made responsible for our salvation. Salvation is defined as the deliverance from the power and effects of sin. Yahweh, in Genesis, placed creation in a perfect Kingdom void of the exploitations of a worldview. The only view was the Kingdom view that was invisible but made visible in purity to a purely created creature. In this, creation is the light of their Creator; we are walking in the light that is placed as a lamp unto our feet and a light unto our pathway. This isn't a mystery; this has become a manipulation based on the fall of man. He cannot and will not dispel himself as an enemy of YAHWEH; man has chosen darkness over the light treasures.

The beautiful outcome of the fallen empires of man is based on their dilemmas. Just as the Jews and Gentiles were taught in error, so deceptive men and women of our present-day are continuing in the fall, repeating the mistakes of their ancestors. We have all fallen short of the glory of God presented in scripture; understanding God's glory and why we fell is based on self-examination. Have we, as the creation of The Most High, come into a full understanding that we are the created beings?

This means that our light treasure within has been manipulated by the fall of man; we are convinced that Yahweh is wrong, and we are right. This leads us to a reprobate mindset. Our light has been exchanged for power, money, and into the outwardly fleshly worship of the material realm. We cannot and will not see the visible Kingdom on earth. Yeshua placed us as the receivers of the light with wisdom so that we may press forward in the middle of our invocation, to comprehend the mystery of the Invisible God and HIS redemption from deception of them of the Left, who think one way, those of them of the Middle who think another way, and those of the Right who force their religion and worldviews in all ways. But before all these ways, He will give them (disciples) the mysteries of the three Baptisms--the Baptism of Water, the Baptism of Fire, and the Baptism of the Holy Spirit. Moreover, He will give them the Mystery of Withdrawing the Malice or Naughtiness (κακία) of the Rulers.

Κακία is defined as evil, malice, naughtiness, and wickedness; each is defined as a blockage to the light treasure and must be eradicated from the humus temple, which are our bodies. Evil is defined as naughtiness, wickedness. Malice means to be ill-willed, to desire to injure. Wicked is defined as not to be ashamed to break the laws, evil trouble. All these definitions play hand in hand to create the behaviors we see before us in the realm in which we live. God has placed His remnant in the midst of these spirits to shed light as a method to deprive these spirits of spreading darkness throughout the world.

But they must remember that, when they, in turn, give these mysteries to others, they must command them not to swear falsely, nor even to swear at all; neither to fornicate nor commit adultery; neither to steal nor covet other men's goods; neither to love silver nor gold, nor invoke the names of the evil Rulers or of their angels for any purpose; not to rob, nor to curse, nor calumniate falsely, nor to rail, but to let their yea be yea and their nay; in a word, they must fulfill the good commandments of God through Moses.

The disciples remind Jesus that His first gift had been that they should be taught the mysteries of the Treasure of Light within them, the greater, which are above these lower mysteries of which He has spoken. The disciples have now abandoned all things in the world and have kept all the commandments but have now followed Jesus towards the greater enigma for these years. Jesus assures them that He will further give them the mysteries of the Light-treasure; they will understand the Light-treasure and the way of their invocation, so that they may pass through their spaces of wisdom, which bestows upon them all the parts of the Mystery of the Forgiveness of Sins; this Mystery transmutes the soul into pure light, so that it may be received into the Light of lights.

Such souls have already inherited the Kingdom of God while still on earth; they have their share of the powers they confer in the Light-treasure and are immortal in the site of Yahweh and at death when they leave the body, and until their souls arrive at the Gates of the Light-treasure. And as the Gates are opened to them, and they are given passage, all these mysteries Jesus promises to give to His disciples are truths that they may be called "Children of the Fullness (Plērōma) perfected in all mysteries."

This is a direct invocation of the scriptures as it relates to the Father as the true light in the Son. There are direct similarities of the passages made by the scriptures of the Bible that support the light treasures; however, in this Gnosis account, it gives a vivid account of the love Yahweh has in store for His creation based on Jesus the Logos and the light He has brought into the world. In this light, Jesus is the Son of man and the Son of God based on the mysteries He reveals to the elect. Man is the love creation of the invisible God, and the light in Christ is the gift that reveals this light to the souls of the believer.

The accounts given in this dialogue have no account of affliction towards the reader, only detailed explanations of the Gnosis in these passages, only the interaction of Jesus and the disciples that, in some depth, explains the fulfillment of Jesus according to the will of the Father, which is the truth of light that exists in God's creation (Yahweh's invisible light). The teaching in the Gnosis is indwelled, based on the teacher (Jesus) to recognize those whom the Father draws to him, and His teachings perfect themselves based on those who are obedient in Light, hearing the calling to be saved from the rulers of the earth and their unlimited abilities to entrap the spirits of the created in God. The invisibility of God is the purifying light that indwells all earthly souls and delivers them from the blemishes that this life placed upon the flesh; Yahweh's redemptive power overcomes this by creating a Race of Gnosis apologetics, which He places in the Word, which are free of the stains of this world.

As we ride out life's pathway, there will be a few truths that will galvanize the flesh because humans have been placed in a methodology that weakens their flesh. They believe what the masses believe, and this is to their demise. Accolades are given to Christians in societies to strengthen the religious system from which it was built. Yeshua chose men and women who were followers of ignorance, who didn't know any better than that of their cultural design, but in their ignorance, they desired to see the light when it came upon them, so much so that they dropped everything and followed a "Truth" they had never met. We're living in the latter days. We're filled with our cultures, church complex, and self-confidence, whether we will admit it or not. We look just like our culture, sound like them, and are fulfilling the culture's desire. We've been introduced to their forms of culture.

We are in the same situation as the disciples, working, surviving in a system that had conformed them. In modern times, this cultural deviance has proclaimed victory over its cultures. They have trained the people in a system so that when they have grown and matured into it, they will not depart from it. In return, the system has done what is planned in the beginning, to make its people slaves to the cultures in which they were brought into. We have become slaves with no true master. We know not of our true Messiah because we know not of the visible kingdom on earth, so we shall perish in this culture designed by Judaism, Greco Roman Catholicism, and Islamic traditions.

Yeshua, Yahweh in the flesh, recognized the affliction of a downtrodden creature called man. Just as in the Genesis account, HE heard the cries of affliction from the Hebrews from the earthly realm that was a stench to HIS nostrils in Heaven and sent forward his servant Moses, guided by the Holy Ghost to deliver HIS remnant from a culture of slavery. We are not the slaves of affliction in our current day, nor are we the bloodline of Ishmael, but we are that of Isaac; we are children of promise. The promise reinstates and secures us with the security that, if we search our hearts and minds for the truth, then we will see the light of the true Messiah. These treasures are the promise given to the twelve Hebrew disciples who set aside their cultural teachings, gave up the traditions of religion, and followed the Messiah's teachings of the light treasures that laid in future wisdom, and in this measure of wisdom, they rediscovered the truth of light that was placed in them by Yahweh at the beginning of time, which in return glorified the remnant of Yahweh for eternity. We trust and believe that we will all witness the spiritual rebirth of the invisible nature of Yahweh in our lifetime in these humus temples created by the "Most High."

Chapter 10

Divine Ranks

The comments concerning the "Light treasures" seem to imply the statements made in chapter nine about the "divine ranks" of spiritual beings without bodies (angels) that was produced by Dionysius The Areopagite, which somewhat preclude a pathway through the light that each choir of spiritual (angelic) hierarchies as "Light Treasurers" or power over each choir must traverse.

The word angel is anthropomorphism, a concept invented for representation by a deity, in this case, Catholicism. Dionysius's name appears in the bible in Acts 17:34 along with a group of believers (Areopagus) in Athens Greece; they were witnessing the demise of the church in Jerusalem that was being transformed into the Roman Catholic Empire. The interesting dispute came about when these Epicurean and Stoic philosophers (Acts 17:16) couldn't conceive Paul's message about Jesus and the resurrection.

Paul was invited to a meeting, along with a group called the Areopagus (Acts 17:19). This group was considered "Mystical Theologians," but based on the content of Dionysius's divine names of the Celestial Hierarchy, they seem to resemble many passages of the OT, and the NT passages (that had not been written to any great extent at that time in the OT nor NT) as they relate to the throne of God and the ranks of spiritual beings (angels) in scripture.

We will find here that there is a relationship to the truth of the invisible light God has placed in His creation throughout the scripture. The human intellectual mind can connect to Yahweh's positive analogous names or terms such as The Power, Everlasting Father, Prince of Peace, Eternal, Love, Universal Being, ABBA, assuming these are limited forms of communicating the incommunicable attributes of the invisible nature of Yahweh. For example, let's define each choir and its relationship in reference to Yahweh and our realm of understanding. Remember, we as children of the Most High are given the spirit of deviation to depart from the established standards given by the physical, intellectual, or moral end; we are spiritually created by the breath of EL ELYON, which elevates on physical and spiritual measures.

In the past, many of us have witnessed the presence of spiritual beings. They can be described as celestial bodies, which are defined with bodily outlines but no physical attributes, nothing that can be described as humanistic. The truth is housed in our dirt bodies and expounded through divination and meditational methodology. We must understand that Yahweh speaks through dream states just as HE did with the Prophets through the HOLY Spirit. Each of these choirs listed below could possibly have come in the form of the Holy Ghost that presided upon the temple of the human creature, which altered their consciousness where their surroundings are perceived as surreal in a dream occurring during certain sleep phases or while awake out of the body while asleep in dream sequences. The outcome is left to those who research these occurrences and witness these forms of spiritual realities.

Once again, history is filled with unexplained gaps as it relates the interpretation of these divine ranks, but we have been given the wisdom and glorification to overcome the pseudo-spiritual phenomenon as they have been presented to us in this realm of understanding. Yahweh has the power to invoke our temples at any given time as the Spirit is adduced at Yahweh's command.

First Choir:	**Second Choir:**	**Third Choir:**
1. Seraphim	4. Dominations	7. Principalities
2. Cherubim	5. Virtues	8. Archangels
3. Thrones	6. Powers	9. Angels

Now the three Great Rulers that are within all these Invisibles held the souls of creation hostage in spiritually created cages or psychological induced trauma. No one can pass beyond the light treasures until he has received the mystery of the forgiveness of sins, but, continuing the Master's design, they are not to fear on this account, for there is no place of punishment in those spaces, for their indwellers received the mysteries that lay ahead. These divine names and what are coined as "Mystical Theology" treats the natural effects of what is ruminating through our prayers as a prelude. In which, we have contemplated based on the lack of developed senses and intelligible forms of assessment while praying to prepare for the experience of light that is void from the divine darkness of the Three Great Rulers, which are the Rulers of Macedonia. These rulers have occupied our intelligence while existing within this realm, which started in 496 B.C.

Once again, read this carefully and recall the biblical reference and spiritual precepts that are present within your temple given by Yahweh.

Seraphim: These are the Spiritual Beings (angels) that come first and are closest to the throne of God. They exist in the uppermost part of the hierarchy, and their very name means ardor. They are said to encircle the throne, existing on the love emanated by God and unceasingly chanting the Trisagion, "Holy, holy, holy..." This burning love keeps them ever close to God's Throne, and they bear love and light to the lesser choirs of angels. It is also this fiery love that gives them the term fiery serpents.

In this form of fiery serpents, it is said that the light they give off is so intense that not even other divine beings may look upon them. There is said to be four of these angelic beings. They are listed as the four holy beasts in the book of Revelation and are described as angels with four faces and six wings.

> *"The name Seraphim clearly indicates their ceaseless and eternal revolution about Divine Principles, their heat and keenness, the exuberance of their intense, perpetual, tireless activity, and their elevated and energetic assimilation of those below, kindling them and firing them to their own heat, and wholly purifying them by burning and all- consuming flame; and by the unhidden, unquenchable, changeless, radiant and enlightening power, dispelling and destroying the shadows of darkness."* Quote from Dionysius the Areopagite

The bible is vague on this topic but picks up on the topic in the book of Isaiah 6:2-3 NIV.
"Seraphim stood above Him, each having six wings; with two he covered his face, and with two he covered his feet, and with two he flew. And one called out to another and said, "Holy, Holy, Holy, is the Lord of hosts; the whole earth is full of His glory."

To be Holy means to be set apart and seen as sacred. This describes The Most High in the invocation of Yahweh's Holiness. The flame of the burning bush that spoke to Moses was that of a Seraphim encounter. In this encounter, Yahweh spoke out through the blue flames to inform Moses that he was standing on Holy ground that was set apart for I AM.

Cherubim: Second to only the seraphim, their name signifies "fullness of knowledge." Characterized by a deep insight into God's secrets, the Cherubim hold the knowledge of God, and they truly possess the fullness of the divine science of heaven. *"It is also they who are often sent to earth with the greatest of tasks; the expulsion of Man from the Garden of Eden and the Annunciation of Yeshua as the incarnated of The Most High were both performed by Cherubim."*

They enlighten the lesser choirs of angels and are to them the Voice of Divine Wisdom. They are described as the charioteers of God, steering the Ophanim. Contrary to paintings on greeting cards and new age book covers, the cherubim are not depicted as fat, winged babies. Instead, they are described as sphinx-like creatures in Assyrian lore, or the angels gracing the Ark of the Covenant and Solomon's temple in biblical terms.

> *"The name Cherubim denotes their power of knowing and beholding God, their receptivity to the highest Gift of*

> *Light, their contemplation of the Beauty of the Godhead in Its First Manifestation, and that they are filled by participation in Divine Wisdom, and bounteously outpour to those below them from their own fount of wisdom."*

Quote from Dionysius the Areopagite

Thrones: Form the last choir of the first hierarchy, which is closest to the Divine Majesty. They are also known as the Ophanim. The primary function of these angles is to be God's chariot, but they are also noted as meting out God's judgment. Their main characteristics are submission and peace; however, they act with impartialness and humility to bring about the desires of the Lord.

Having the most bizarre physical appearance of the celestial host, they are described as great wheels, covered with a great many eyes and glowing with light. One explanation given for this (besides them acting as God's chariot) is that they mark the end of the first Choir, where the emanations of God begin to take on more material forms and, as such, exist in a state of transition. God's spirit is conveyed in a certain manner to these angels, who in turn, pass on the message to men and the inferior angels.

> *"The name of the most glorious and exalted Thrones denotes that which is exempt from and untainted by any base and earthly thing, and the super mundane ascent up the steep. For these have no part in that which is lowest, but dwell in fullest power, immovably and perfectly established in the Most High, and receive the Divine Immanence above all passion and matter, and manifest God, being attentive open to divine participations."*
>
> Quote from Dionysius the Areopagite

Dominations: Are so called because "they rule over all the angelic orders charged with the execution of the commands of the Great Monarch." They are also known as the Hashmallim, whose purpose is to regulate the duties of the lower angels. They act as a form of middle management between the upper choir and the lower. Receiving their orders from the seraphim and cherubim, these bright spirits make known to us the commands of God and ensure the cosmos remains in order. Their main virtue is zeal for the maintenance of the King's authority. Only on very rare occasions do they reveal themselves to mortals; instead, they quietly concern themselves with the details of existence.

> *"The name given to the holy Dominions signifies, I think, a certain unbounded elevation to that which is above,*

freedom from all that is of the earth, and from all inward inclination to the bondage of discord, a liberal superiority to harsh tyranny, an exemption from degrading servility and from all that is low: for they are untouched by any inconsistency. They are true Lords, perpetually aspiring to true lordship, and to the Source of lordship, and they providentially fashion themselves and those below them, as far as possible, into the likeness of true lordship. They do not turn towards vain shadows, but wholly give themselves to that true Authority, forever one with the Godlike Source of lordship." Quote from Dionysius the Areopagite

Virtues: Also known as the Malakim and the Tarshishim, they carry out the orders issued by the Dominations. They also have two main tasks: to maintain the aspects of the natural world and to bestow blessings upon the material world. They are attributed with having strength, and their assistance should be sought to combat the enemies of salvation. Their primary duty is to: *"preside over the movements of the celestial bodies as well as events of weather including rain, snow, wind, and the like."*

Their secondary duty is to: *"take the orders given to them and, in turn, convert them into miracles for God's favored."* Bouden states: *"It is through them also that God governs the seasons, the* visible heavens and the elements in general, although angels of the lower hierarchy have charge of them."

> "The name of the holy Virtues signifies a certain powerful and unshakable virility welling forth into all their Godlike energies; not being weak and feeble for any reception of the divine Illuminations granted to it; mounting upwards in the fullness of power to assimilation with God; never falling away from the Divine Life through its own weakness, but ascending unwaveringly to the superessential Virtue which is the Source of virtue: fashioning itself, as far as it may, in virtue; perfectly turned towards the Source of virtue, and flowing forth providentially to those below it, abundantly filling them with virtue."

Quote from Dionysius the Areopagite

Powers: Believed to be "the favorites among mortals," they hold one of the most dangerous tasks, maintaining the border between Heaven and Earth. Constantly on guard for demonic attacks, the powers act like an elite guard. They are appointed in a special way to fight against the evil spirits and to defeat any wicked plans.

> *"When we see storms gathering either in the Church or in the State, machinations to resist those who are working for the glory of God, extraordinary conspiracies to defeat some great good which is being planned for some diocese, city or country, then it is that we ought to perform frequent devotions in honor of these Powers of heaven, that they may overturn and destroy all the might and miserable plotting of hell."* (Boudon)

During heavenly warfare, they are a major line of defense. They are also tasked with guarding the celestial byways between the two realms and ensuring that souls, which leave the mortal world, reach heaven safely. Perhaps not surpassingly, given their proximity to the nether regions, there are more angels from the ranks of the powers listed as fallen than from any other member of the hierarchy.

> *"The name of the holy Powers, co-equal with the Divine Dominions and Virtues, signifies an orderly and unconfined order in the divine receptions, and the regulation of intellectual and supermundane power which never debases its authority by tyrannical force, but is irresistibly urged onward in due order to the Divine. It*

> *beneficently leads those below it, as far as possible, to the Supreme Power, which is the Source of Power, which it manifests after the manner of Angels in the well-ordered ranks of its own authoritative power."*
>
> Quote from Dionysius the Areopagite

Principalities: They are the head of the final choir and preside over the third hierarchy. They guide and protect the world's nations, towns, and cities, directly watch over the mortal world and are executive in regard to the visible world of men. Religion and politics are also guarded by them and, "as such, they are assumed to be given more freedom to act than the lesser angels below them and are responsible for carrying out divine acts concerning their area of jurisdiction."

Finally, they are given the task of managing the duties of the angels. St. Thomas says of them: "The execution of the angelic ministries consists of announcing divine things." Now, in the execution of any action, there are beginners and leaders; this-the leadership-belongs to the Principalities.

> *"The name of the Celestial Principalities signifies their Godlike princeliness and authoritativeness in an Order which is holy and most fitting to the princely Powers, and*

> *that they are wholly turned towards the Prince of Princes, and lead others in princely fashion, and that they are formed, as far as possible, in the likeness of the Source of Principality, and reveal Its super essential order by the good Order of the princely Powers."* Quote from Dionysius the Areopagite

Archangels: Although they are normally described as important or special angels, here, the term is used as the second to last rank in the celestial hierarchy. Archangels are entrusted with the more important missions to men. They act as the leaders in the divine army during the battle and protect the Church under the leadership of St. Michael. They serve as guardians of guardians of great personages, such as the Holy Father, Cardinals, Bishops, Rulers of States; this includes others with special work to do for the glory of God upon earth. Finally, they are charged with overseeing the duties of the angels.

> *"The confusion about the collective celestial rank of archangels and archangels arises from the ancient Hebraic way of defining angels, which was a simple angel and archangel. It was not until later that the hierarchy was defined, and many of the angels previously named as simply archangels were given new posts."*

> *"The choir of the holy Archangels is placed in the same threefold Order as the Celestial Principalities; for, as has been said, there is one Hierarchy and Order which includes these and the Angels. But since each Hierarchy has first middle and last ranks, the holy Order of Archangels, through its middle position, participates in the two extremes, being joined with the most holy Principalities and with the holy Angels."*
>
> Quote from Dionysius the Areopagite

Angels: To bring to a close the last choir in the hierarchy, they are ever ready to go wherever the will of God sends them. They have two major tasks: First, they are the ordinary messengers sent to men to watch over mortals in a more direct manner than the principalities. They tend to mirror the goodness of God and direct it toward mortals. They help to protect and keep us safe from demonic attack, households and individual souls, instead of entire nations.

Second, they carry God's word to mankind and act as messengers and couriers to both God and the upper ranks of angel kind. With a true sense of values, they minister to all, ranging from sinners to the good and just. In Hebrew, they are called mal'akh, meaning, "messenger"; in Persian, the word is

Angaros or "courier." Above all, they realize that serving God in any capacity is a very great honor.

> *"For the Angels, as we have said, fill up and complete the lowest choir of all the Hierarchies of the Celestial Intelligence since they are the last of the Celestial Beings possessing the angelic nature.*
>
> *And they, indeed, are more properly named Angels by us than are those of a higher rank because their choir is more directly in contact With manifested and mundane things."*

Quote from Dionysius the Areopagite

The highest Order, as we have read, being in the foremost place near the Hidden One is the Seraphim, which must be regarded as hierarchically ordering in a hidden manner as the second Order; the second Order of Dominions, Virtues and Powers, leads the Principalities, Archangels and Angels more manifestly than the first Hierarchy but in a more hidden manner than the Order below it; the revealing Order of the Principalities, Archangels and Angels presides one through the other over the human hierarchies so that their elevation and turning to God and their communion and union with Him may be in order; moreover, that the procession from God, beneficently granted to all the Hierarchies, and visiting them all in common, maybe with the most holy order.

"Accordingly, the Word of God has given our hierarchy into the care of Angels, for Michael is called Lord of the people of Judah, and other Angels are assigned to other peoples. For the Most High established the boundaries of the nations according to the number of the Angels of God."[23]

These triple-powered entities could be the relationship to each "heading of the three choirs," which started with the powers closest to God, which are the Seraphim, Domination, and then the Principalities. These line up as the first of each of the choirs of angels that release the light passages all the way down to the angels, which are below the Archangels. We who consist of humus and spirit are below the angels, the central truths related to us receiving salvation, Yahweh has determined this (our salvation),

"That in the dispensation of the fullness of time HE (The Father) might gather together in one all things in the Spirit, both which are in heaven, and which are on earth; even in Him." -Ephesians 1:10

When we examine these choirs of Spiritual Beings, we should pray in discernment that we, as humans, are given the gift of insight, wisdom, and glorification. In this realm, we are deceived by a fallen conqueror called evil man, who has enslaved our dirt bodies and oppressed the trueness of our light. That within this vessel, the light has overcome anything this evil has put forward and can be overcome by truth and righteousness. As we transcend in these dirt jumpsuits, we are destined to start and finish the race on earth.

"The race is not for the swift nor the battle to the strong, nor does food come to the wise or wealth to the brilliant or favor to the learned; but time and chance happen to them all" **- Ecclesiastes 9:11**

"When I was a child, I talked like a child, I thought like a child, I reasoned like a child. When I became a man, I put the ways of childhood behind me." **-1 Corinth. 13:11**

"I was young, and now I am old, yet I have never seen the righteous forsaken or their children begging for bread." **- Psalms 37:25**

In these Biblical passages, we can relate to that which we once were, and where we are now, and as it relates to what enters in our humus temple as man's definitions of Christianity. Our bodies are spiritually conditioned to discern truth from falsehood. Our fleshly encrustation is protected by the full armor coverage created of Invisible Nature of Yahweh that protects and deflects evil influence and should cover the internal spirit. We should see through the choirs listed that this is the Roman Catholic Empire that has subjugated the thoughts of the heavenly realm and instituted their own deity.

"You dear children are from God and have overcome them because the one who is in you is greater than the one who is in the world." **-1 John 4:4**

In this, which will one day prove that we will be outside the constraints of its fleshly oppressed temple body, and we will be eternally within the celestial (spatial) body created to transcend time infinitely. When we reach the immortal, heavenly, spiritual, and become sublime, our mortal will no longer exist. Who is anyone to say that the vision given in this chapter of the divine ranks has no validity? It may be true but outside of the way in which man has presented it to the masses.

To have a dream epiphany places one to experience a sudden and striking realization, manifestation, or striking appearance of enlightenment. It can be applied in any situation in which an enlightening realization allows a problem or situation to be understood from a deeper perspective. This can be considered a leap into the unknown to bring clarity to something that we may encounter, such as challenges relating to spiritual warfare in our realm of substance. We were appointed for this very purpose, to wear these bodies, to encounter this life.

We must recognize we don't have a spirit; we are spirits that have been predestined to a holy calling, to justify the invisible spirit of Yahweh, so that we may be glorified outside the measures of a fallen kingdom here on earth.

We must rediscover what has been lost. Fallen man has manipulated the Kingdom on earth. Yeshua never preached any religion, culture, or entitled groups that should rule the Kingdom Principles put in place by "The Most High." The truth is placed in all creation, and we have the responsibility as light bearers to bring this truth back into a focused reality. There are truths in these choirs that place us in motion to recognize there is a designation surrounding its messages, but the truth must come from the invisible nature that exists in the presentation of the truth and righteousness Kingdom in the earthly realm, so that the light within our temples will mesh with the truths of those who have been predestined to provide the messages of truths in the Kingdom of Yahweh that exist within us.

Chapter 11
Yahweh Directs the Human Spirit

Everyone will be placed in the Light. This is a forgone conclusion, a principle, and a promise made by God. *"The one who comes from above is above is above all"* -John 3:31 (NIV).

The invisibility of God's light will return to Him not void of what He placed in the humus flesh in the beginning. Our passage starts with the angels interceding on behalf of Jesus, *"For the Lord himself will come down from heaven, with a loud command, with the voice of the archangel and with the trumpet call of God, and the dead in Christ will rise first. After that, we who are still alive and are left will be caught up together with them in the clouds to meet the Lord in the air. And so we will be with the Lord forever. Therefore encourage each other with these words"* -1 Thess. 4:16-18 (NIV).

In this message, Paul speaks and teaches to the Thessalonians of the coming of Jesus. Dionysius Lines up the pathway in his analogy and the message of salvation sums up the same, which leads us to God's invisible nature from His heavenly throne all the way to where we are and to where he will deliver us back to, which is through Yahweh's invisible nature and His ability to deliver on a promise made long ago. Understand that Yahweh is preparing each and every one of us as His followers to be a testimony to the true Word that is salvation in the believers.

Understanding Yahweh's position as being sovereign in His invisibility adds to the notion of what is expected of the creatures, Praise! God, in His invisibility, produced a magnificent miracle. He made from the dirt a model of a humus being. This model was empty and was without life as the scripture depicts in Genesis chapter 1:27-28:

"God created man in His own image, in the image of God he created him; male and female he created them. God blessed them and said to them, "Be fruitful and increase in number; fill the earth and subdue it. Rule over the fish of the sea and the birds of the air and every living creature that moves on the ground."

Here is the invisible nature of God passing unto the creature an invitation to have the authority to enjoy an earthly kingdom that is filled with everything life has to offer. What is discovered here is that God is an invisible, Sovereign Spirit that is speaking life into a dirt creature by regenerating the dirt through the breath of His word. The mere dirt is without form or servitude, but God provided a creative purpose for the humus and decreed the humus as His own image. In Genesis 2:7, *"God breathed into (His creative being) his nostrils the breath of life, and the man became a living being."*

This man (Jesus) had the invisible spirit of God inside his dirt body; just as Jesus was called the "Son of Man," Jesus had a dirt body with a spirit of atonement for the expiation for sin, the reconciliation of God and mankind through Yeshua's teachings.

"What is man, that thou art mindful of him, and the son of man, that thou visits him?"
-Psalms 8:4

"Let thy hand be upon the man of thy right hand, upon the son of man whom thou madest strong for thyself." **-Psalms 80:17**

The word Son of God has to do with the deity of Christ. He is truly God. The relationship between the Father and the Son must be understood in a figurative sense. The word Son in our own human description has to do with the identity of nature and mutual affection. The only begotten Son means the only person in relation to the Father. Yeshua taught in the same nature with his internal spirit that he is of God.

There is no inferiority in the Spirit, as the Spirit is the Messiah, and the Messiah has no inferiority. The Messiah is with the same nature as the Father; the Messiah and the Father are, in some respect, distinct from each other.

The Father is not the Son, and the Son is not the Father, but they are one in divine nature. The Father and the Son are one, just as we are the daughters and sons of The Most High. Also, there is a mutual affection between them. Just like a father loves his son, as if he has only one son, in the same way, the Father loves the Son.

The word Son of Man has to do with His humanity. The word man has plurality, meaning all human creation. God becoming like the image of a man, is all-inclusive. He is truly a man, at the same time, distinguished from all other men. He is the perfect man. He is the one who represents his people as the spiritual creation in the perfect Kingdom on earth. The second Adam, God-man, God manifests in the flesh.

The key statement here is Yeshua is the one who represents his people to the Yahweh. Yeshua was sent as reparation for a wrong or injury made to the flesh. The spirit had been afflicted based on the manipulation of the flesh, which had become an enduring generational curse throughout time (Idolatry). Yahweh understood this, the Yeshua knew this, the Holy Spirit was vested in this, and they (The Triune nature) transcended time, allowing men and women who were spiritually filled by the Holy Spirit to investigate the wisdom of the invisibility of Yahweh, and an understanding that God desired that all would come to understand the invisible nature that had been placed in His creatures (Humans) that they too would figure out that He was coming, transcending time in the spirit to provide the ("Keys") solution to the fall of man.

"The idea of a transcendent God has roots both in Judaism and in Neoplatonic philosophy. The Old Testament, for example, records a prohibition against idols, and this can be interpreted as an attempt to emphasize the wholly "otherness" of God, which cannot be represented physically. In this context, God is so utterly alien that it's wrong to attempt to portray it in any sort of concrete fashion. Neoplatonic philosophy, in a similar manner, emphasized the idea that God is so pure and perfect that it completely transcended all of our categories, ideas, and concepts.

The idea of an imminent God can also be traced to both Judaism and other Greek philosophers. Many stories in the Old Testament depict a God who is very active in human affairs and the working of the universe.

Christians, especially mystics, have often described a God who works within them and whose presence they can perceive immediately and personally. Various Greek philosophers have also discussed the idea of a God who is somehow united with our souls, such that this union can be understood and perceived by those who study and learn enough." Austin Cine

In the fulfillment in Christ, our concerns should be what the Holy Spirit did for us throughout the historical gospels. The event in fulfilling the promise of the OT, and what God's "Word" and his Spirit does in us as we carry this light of the spirit that fuels our faith and connects us to the truths presented by The Holy Spirit that was given in Yeshua as He ascended to the clouds.

With the end times consummation upon us, there is glorification within us that is invisible. Man sees the outer shell, but Yeshua saw the inner light spirit and will return in pure glory to judge the living and the dead and bring into light the invisible spirit and the fullness of The Kingdom of Yahweh. The way that distinguishes the work done by Yeshua, for us, is in us, with us; it is simplistic in the light of God, distinguishing our Justification, the past, our sanctification in the present, and our glorification, which is His reconciliation through future events that indicate we have been regenerated by the parables given in scripture pertaining to His saving grace and mercy, which will transcend as light in an invisible spiritual nature.

Our notions about the nature and integration of passages from the Bible may need to be altered in the light of our continuation towards examining the text in reference to our existence. The error of historical events and structural framework of the Bible events have distorted the witness accounts, which in return have placed a clay jar over our light and its hidden truths; the light can't be seen. This is true for the invisible nature of the spirit of God in us. The healing power of redemptive love is the historical witness of the Bible from Genesis to the Revelation, which reveals the Kingdom of God that is truly contained in the light-invisibility of the spirit of His creation.

Yeshua transcended time to reveal this to the creatures as the Son of Man; He was truly able to perform the miracles because He had the power as the Word of God to do the things His Father told Him to do. At the core of the "Triune Power" is the kingdom of God, and through the work of the Son, we who seek to have a relationship with the light of Yahweh will be strengthened towards maturing in the invisibility faith,

"Now faith is being sure of what we hope for and certain of what we do not see" (Hebrews 11:1)

Our primary faith response is Yahweh, who we can't see through a nurturing understanding of the invisible nature of the persons of God, the transcending power, the authority placed in us the creature, and the consequential nature of our light nature in relationship to the light that was in

Yeshua, and the eternal relationship of the universal love that God has placed before His creation.

The ultimate purpose is for us to take the leap of faith into the light of Yeshua, the flesh encrusted body incarnated by the invisible nature of Yahweh.

"There is a judge for the one who rejects me and does not accept my words; the very words I have spoken will condemn them at the last day. For I did not speak on my own, but the Father who sent me commanded me to say all that I have spoken. I know that His command leads to eternal life. So whatever I say is just what the Father has told me to say" -**John 12:50 (NIV)**

There is a significant verse that sums up God's creation, surpassing a point beyond the limits that restricts the amount of information that is permissible or possible within this syndrome. What is being preached doesn't legitimize nor effectively reach the invisibility of the spirit within; however, the Holy Spirit knows exactly what the creator has set in place. The world doesn't have to rely on science, politics, religion, or philosophy to acquire the governing wisdom of Yahweh.

"For to us, a child is born, to us, a son is given, and the government will be on his shoulders. And he will be called Wonderful Counselor, Mighty God, Everlasting Father, Prince of Peace" -**Isa. 9:6 (NIV)**

God's elect through Yeshua already knows the light visibility within, and we will not dispute His existence; however, unlike those who deliberately ignore the evidence that is plainly seen, will continue to miss the attributes that make the invisibility of Yahweh visible in this realm. Our senses are in place to understand the truth, the light, and the way. Like the nocturnal creatures of the night who can only operate in the darkness and sleep during the light of the daytime, resembling the human who is left in the dark, he willfully seeks darkness in impiety and injustice, yet by the grace of the light, the invisibility of Yahweh it was given; in mercy, it was sown. This is the "Amazing Grace."

In an article written by Joseph Herrin (6-18-03), he extrapolates his perspective from his invisible light,

"Understanding the relationship between Spirit and breath was building block number one in coming to understand the relationship between Father, Son, and Spirit. The next building block came as I tried to answer the question regarding where man would look for his spirit."

"We know that a spirit is invisible to the natural senses. We cannot take a picture of a man's spirit. Not even an x-ray will show the spirit of man. Our spirit was formed

in the image of the invisible God, and our spirit is likewise invisible. Yet we talk about seeing the spirit of another person very often. We might say, "He has a kind spirit," or "She has a bitter spirit."

"A commonly heard expression is "He is the spirit and image of his father" (Some areas have corrupted this expression and lost its true sense as they say, "He is the spitting image of his father." "Spitting" is a slang corruption of "spirit and").

If we do not see another person's spirit, then how do we recognize their spirit? It is our words that express what is inside of us. Yeshua said:
"That which proceeds out of the man, that is what defiles the man.
For from within, out of the heart of men, proceed the evil thoughts, fornications, thefts, murders, adulteries, deeds of coveting and wickedness, as well as deceit, sensuality, envy, slander, pride, and foolishness.

All these evil things proceed from within and defile the man" -Mark 7:20-23

"The things that are in man's spirit will come out of his mouth. By listening to another person's speech, we can discern their spirit. We can easily tell if a father and a son have the same spirit by listening to their words. Are they both hateful? Are they both compassionate? Whatever is in their spirit will be revealed in their speech."

"Now a light began to come on inside when I was led to consider how man forms of words. We speak as our breath is exhaled and passes over our vocal cords. We only speak as we exhale, and we do not speak while inhaling. This is no accident. It is by Divine design. Yahweh is teaching us something about Himself in this simple example of the speech of man. We cannot see man's spirit until his spirit is exhaled and forms words. A man's spirit is revealed in his words."

"In the same way, we cannot see God, who is Spirit until He breathes out a Word.

He who is the blessed and only Sovereign, the King of kings and Lord of lords, who alone possesses immortality and dwells in unapproachable light, whom no man has seen or can see"-1 Timothy 6:15-16

"No one has seen God at any time; the only begotten God who is in the bosom of the Father, He has declared (revealed, expressed) Him" (John 1:18).

"Yahweh is Spirit, and as Spirit, He is invisible to the physical senses of man. Yahweh would remain invisible to man had He not spoken a Word, and this Word is His Son." [26]

"In the beginning was the Word, and the Word was with God, and the Word was God. He was at the beginning with God... And the Word became flesh and dwelt among us, and we saw His glory, glory as of the only begotten from the Father, full of grace and truth." -John 1:1, 2, 14

"Even as man's spirit is seen through his words, so Yahweh who is Spirit can only be seen through His Word, which is Yeshua the Son. In Yeshua Yahweh has fully expressed Himself. To see the Son is to see the invisible Father."

Philip said to Him, "Lord, show us the Father, and it is enough for us." Yeshua said to him, "Have I been so long with you, and yet you have not come to know Me, Philip? He who has seen Me has seen the Father; how can you say, "Show us the Father?"
-John 14:8-9

"As we look at Yahweh's design of man and the production of speech, we learn a great truth about the Father, Son, and Spirit. The spirit of man is invisible, but it is who the man essentially is. The character of a man is bound up in his spirit. His thoughts are formed in his spirit. Yet neither the character nor the thoughts of a man are evident until they are given expression. The chief way

that God has designed man to express himself is through speech, and our speech is generated as we exhale the breath that is within us, and this breath is given shape as it passes over our vocal cords."

"What a picture this is of the Trinity. Yahweh is also invisible, for He is Spirit. His character and His thoughts remain invisible until they are given expression. His expression is His Son, who is called "the Word of God," and this Word was formed as the Spirit, or Divine Breath of God moved."

"The angel answered and said to [Mary], "The Holy Spirit will come upon you, and the power of the Most High will overshadow you; and for that reason, the holy Child shall be called the Son of God."
-Luke 1:35

John testified, saying, "I have seen the Spirit descending as a dove out of heaven, and He remained upon Him. I did not recognize Him, but He who sent me to baptize in water said to me, 'He upon whom you see the Spirit descending and remaining upon Him, this is the One who baptizes in the Holy Spirit.' I myself have seen and have testified that this is the Son of God."- John 1:32-34

"In these two verses, an important truth is revealed. It required two distinct acts of the Spirit to fully form the Word of God. Yeshua could not begin His ministry of declaring who the Father is until the Spirit moved upon Him a second time. He was not yet the full expression of Yahweh until the Spirit descended upon Him and remained. In the same way, man requires two touches from God's Spirit (the Divine Breath) to begin manifesting the character and thoughts of God to the world. We see these two touches from God in the following verses."

"Then when God formed man of dust from the ground, breathed into his nostrils, the breath of life, and man became a living soul." -Genesis 2:7

"So Yeshua said to them again, "Peace be with you; as the Father has sent Me, I also send you." And when He had said this, He breathed on them and said to them, "Receive the Holy Spirit." -John 20:21-22

"Twice the breath of God had to move upon man to make him into God's new creation. With the first breath, man became a living soul. With the second breath, he became a life giving spirit."

"So also it is written, "The first man, Adam, became a living soul." The last Adam became a life-giving spirit. However, the spiritual is not first, but the natural; then the spiritual.

The first man is from the earth, an earthy being, a humus (dirt) being, which is a human being; the second man is from heaven.

As is the earthy man, so also are those who are earthy; and as is heavenly, so also are those who are heavenly.

And just as we have borne the image of the earthly, we shall also bear the image of the heavenly."
-I Corinthians 15:45-49

"As Yahweh breathes, an image is formed, in the same way, that we breathe, and we form words that create an image of our spirit. We have born the image of the earthly, yet we shall also bear the image of the heavenly. At God's first breath, man became a living soul, a natural being that is earthly. At His second breath, man became a life giving spirit, and the image of the heavenly being began to take shape in us."

"This process of being formed into the heavenly image is a process that will continue until the Spirit is fully formed in us."

"But we all, with unveiled face, beholding as in a mirror the glory of the Lord, are being transformed into the same image from glory to glory, just as from the Lord, the Spirit"

-II Corinthians 3:18"

Here we are led to understand the nuisances that many feel. Why is our Lord so unreasonable, and why must His spirit burden us? Mr. Herrin acknowledges this by exposing our invisibility and bringing to surface our "Acts."

We see our image in the flesh, by uncovering the truth of our breath; this reveals our unsanctified words that come from our mouth.

> *"As Yahweh breathes an image is formed, in the same way, that we breathe and we form words that create an image of our earthly spirit. We have born the image of the earthly, yet we shall also bear the image of the heavenly."* 26

This is where the image and nature of the Son Of Man was pronounced as the second coming in the sight of God's creation, to make known to man the truth, the light, and the way. That all who witness the "True and living Word" would be regenerated and sanctified, and the true invisibility of the breath of God would transform the creature, and the righteousness and truth would come from the created creature's breath.

Conclusion:

J.I. Packer answers the question in his interpretation to transcend in our invisible of Yahweh:

"To transcend means "to exist above and independent from; to rise above, surpass, succeed." By this definition, God is the only truly transcendent Being. The "LORD God Almighty" (in Hebrew, El Shaddai) created all things on the earth, beneath the earth and in the heavens above. Yet, He exists above and

independent from them. All things are upheld by His mighty power (Hebrews 1:3), yet He upholds the Spiritual alone. The whole universe exists in Him, and for Him, that He may receive glory, honor, and praise.

Being transcendent, God is both the unknown and unknowable. Yet, God continually seeks to reveal Himself to His creation, i.e., the unknown seeks to be known. Here is a paradox. Being transcendent, God is the incomprehensible Creator existing outside of space and time and thus is unknowable and unsearchable. Neither by an act of our will nor by our own reasoning can we possibly come to understand God or experience Him personally. God wants us to seek to know Him, yet how can the finite possibly know and understand the infinite when our minds and thoughts are so far beneath His (Isaiah 55:8-9)?

Romans 11:33-36 says, **"Oh, the depth of the riches of the wisdom and knowledge of God. How unsearchable his judgments, and his paths beyond tracing out! Who has known the mind of the Lord? Or who has been His counselor? Who has ever given to God, that God should repay him? For from him and through him and to him are all things. To him is the glory forever!"**

Another aspect of God's transcendent nature that places Him beyond the reach of His creation is His holiness and His righteousness. Because of man's proclivity to sin and his desire for wickedness, he is denied the right to enter God's presence. God has no choice but to turn His face away from us like He did with Moses when he asked to see God's glory. God told Moses, *"You cannot see my face, for no one may see my face and live"* (Exodus 33:20). To see the fullness of the glory of God would be too much for any human to bear; it would break the earthen vessel into pieces. The full revelation of God is therefore reserved for the future when all things will be seen as they are, and men will be in a condition to receive them.

The prophet Isaiah realized the necessity of God remaining aloof from His creation: *"All of us have become like one who is unclean, and all our righteous acts are like filthy rags; we all shrivel up like a leaf, and like the wind, our sins sweep us away. No one calls on your name or strives to lay hold of you; for you have hidden your face from us and made us waste away because of our sins"* - *Isaiah 64:6-7.*

A transcendent God must turn His face away, for He is forced by His very righteousness and holiness to keep Himself separate from anything or anyone sinful, impure, unclean, or less than perfect.

However, besides being transcendent, God also possesses immanence (nearness), and it is in His immanence that God chooses to draw near to His creation. This, too, is a paradox.

"Am I only a God nearby," declares the LORD, "and not a God far away? Can anyone hide in secret places so that I cannot see him?" declares the LORD.

"Do I not fill heaven and earth?" declares the LORD
-Jeremiah 23:23-24.

> *"God's transcendent nature strives to keep Him distant and remote from His creation both in space and time. Yet, on the other hand, His immanent nature works to draw Him near to His creation and to sustain the universe. God's love for His creation is so great that we see His immanence overshadowing His transcendence. This becomes clear in His incarnate Spirit, Yeshua, as He breaks through the barrier of sin and separation to draw all mankind back into a close, personal relationship. We see God not only choosing to draw near to His creation but to come personally into the hearts and minds of His people through the indwelling power of His Holy Spirit. This is the miracle of God's transcendence."*

"Now this is observed by Elihu to Job, to encourage him to attend to him without fear, since he was a man, a creature of God, as he was: it may be understood of his spiritual formation, the Spirit of God remakes men, or makes them new men, new creatures; this is done in regeneration, which is the work of the Holy Spirit; hence regeneration, and renewing of the Holy Ghost, are put together; and being a work of almighty power, is proof of the deity of the Spirit of God; it is he that quickens men when dead in trespasses and sins, and makes them alive to God; which appears by their spiritual breathings after divine things, and by the exercise of their spiritual senses, and by their performance of spiritual actions; and now Elihu, being a man regenerated and quickened by the Spirit, might more justly claim the attention of Job, since what he should say was what he had heard, felt, and seen, as a good man, one that had an experience of divine and spiritual things.
Gil's Exposition

The true power of light, which is Yahweh's invisibility, rests, rules, and abides with the flesh of His creation. Our resistance is our earthly stance, which dims our light. The forces of evil rule based on contradictions made in historical events that have shed darkness over the light, but we should rest assured, the light always prevails. Our light is the movement, the momentum of the transcendence of the Holy Spirit that comes upon Yahweh creation. All that is needed is faith; summon the Holy Spirit, give it permission, clean your temple from the inside out, make preparation, reparation, allow a miracle to take place; it shall come as the light in creation to break the stronghold of darkness in all things. Amen!

CHAPTER 12

YAHWEH'S VISIBILITY AS TRUTH

God has placed everything in order in the cosmos and the universe. These things have been put in place for all eternity; nothing shall ever be shifted or removed by man. What God has put together, let no man take apart. When we see nature in its broad sense, everything has its place. Animals have their place. When they venture outside of what God has planned for them, they violate the rules outside of their habitat, and they are dealt with. Sometimes death is the penalty. If not death, then the animal is severely traumatized or maimed and retreats in submissive fear into that environment that God naturally designated as their habitat. This form of survival is prevalent for all God's creatures, even the human creatures. God has placed before all creation His designated boundaries. When God placed everything in order, there was purpose involved. We must first recognize who God is. He is Order in the respect that the *Spirit*

"Art in heaven hollowed be thy name thy kingdom come MY will be done on earth as it is in heaven" -Matt. 6:9 (NIV)

He has placed humanity in a spiritual servitude as a form of eternal protection that we would be invisibly covered for all eternity, with protection from the knowledge of good and evil.

Romans 8:4 depicts God as one who is nurturing, who desires that we are led by the Spirit who is greater than the world, one who is protection against the plantation mentality of this world. We should follow the Spiritual plans placed before us, which are good towards adoption into Yahweh's fold. For God is our Abba and has placed all things into the perfect position, even us, the human creation.

Humans have a dirt body and an internal spirit. God is a Spirit without a dirt body and an infinite universal almighty source, and this spirit incarnated the body of the Yeshua to the degree that the flesh became obedient to the spirit that incarnated it. The incarnated Spirit is what God is, ONE! The all-encompassing "Invisible Spirit" is the breath that has placed all things in perspective by a superlative design, which is in-comprehensive and invisible to the creatures but also assessable by the divine grace given to humans as an initiative or desire to bring their flesh into alignment with their internal spirit; in this, the humus body is one with the spirit, and there is no conflict between them and God. The nature and being of Yahweh go far beyond an advanced, superhuman version of us. Yet Yahweh chose a human vessel to be God in the body of Yeshua.

Yeshua was destined to bring confusion to the heart of mankind. They had sinned beyond their own understanding and continued to look for other ways to sin even more than they had in the past. Jesus had left an impression upon the minds of some of these followers. There were messages of the perilous times that would come. The Bible states this,

"For men shall be lovers of their own selves, covetous, boasters, proud, blasphemers, disobedient to parents, unthankful, unholy, but evil men and seducers shall wax worse and worse, deceiving, and being deceived." - 2 Timothy 3:2

We have become somewhat of a mocked Christian nation reflecting its values from ancient Greece, a rule by one who has absolute power without legal right, and our values and spirit reflect that of an evil insecure form of nationalism of those who have fallen from grace into a nation of oppressive governmental rules that operates under cruel, unreasonable, and arbitrary use of power and control.

In order to find our way out of this insanity put on us by the behavior of man, we need a Savior like Yeshua to show human beings what our invisibility looks like. The life of Jesus matters due to the fact that the life of man is sin, and a life of sin leads to eternal death. Sin has been prevalent since the fall of Adam. God had already placed mercy upon His fallen creation; man couldn't see this and become enthralled with sin and death. Man knew no way out, and although Yahweh spoke of the Messiah in the Torah and Septuagint, He spoke through the prophets of the Old Testament, and the evil man continued to ignore Him. God knew He would have to make an appearance as "I AM" in the flesh to show man the way to salvation. Jesus's life mattered because their stony hearts were a reflection of the sins they carried, and Jesus was the intersection of life to which they needed to yield.

The Lord spoke as a moral agent (The Son Of God) to the effect that He saw past man's ego, sin, and disparities. Jesus wanted man to recognize the perfection that God had incarnated in Him, and that was in the invisible sense, a quality that men and women alike denied based on their cults, which became their culture, and this was them operating in religions based on hearsay. God desires them to turn from sin to repentance, from repentance to regeneration, and then to salvation. This was the glorified promise that Jesus wanted them to be aware of and to surrender their flesh to the invisible internal spirit of Yahweh. In this way, their burdens would be removed, and they would gain peace in a spiritual life within the Kingdom of God. This is why we fall short in this life; it's due to a lack of knowledge of the invisible nature of Yahweh in our lives;

we should truly teach about the kingdom of God just as our Messiah taught.

"But seek first HIS kingdom and HIS Righteousness, and all these things will be given to you as well" -**Matthew 6:33**

Yahweh's invisible nature lives in His creation; we are a spiritual creation, and the invisibility of EL's breath serves as His life force in the creation of all people of all generations in the universe. The existing light view fits nicely with the idea of progressive revelation. Abraham was saved by faith, although the content of what was believed was God's promise about his offspring (Gen. 15:6). Some may reach the objective that, because Abraham had no other special revelation available to him at that time, he knew nothing of Yahweh's eternal light within himself, nor the reflective properties of the dwelling light of the Holy Spirit that would exist in future generations of his bloodline. The analogy is perfect. Apollos had believed "accurately" regarding Jesus but knew only John's baptism (Acts 18:24-26). Other revelations were available at the time, but Apollos did not know it. Thus, it is possible that God judges the individual not by the criterion of what revelation has been given to all mankind up to that time, but by the criterion of what is available to the individual.

Therefore, it is obvious that God has placed in all creation the redemptive light, the invisibility of His general revelation that dwells in all creation whether aware or unaware that He chooses to indwell through the Holy Spirit at any point in time through special revelation, through observation, illusions, or the specific manifestation of that revelation. This within itself defines Yahweh as objective through the lens of His creation, but even more so subjective based on the social and spiritual anthropomorphisms handed down through history. Denying Yahweh as the invisible spirit, giving Him the label that best fits our limited influences of what HE has done in space and time, doesn't change what we have done to move further away from the truths HE has placed in us. Our destructive tendencies only build on the sinfulness presence in our societies and across the globe. Being able to focus internally from within, reviewing our past history, and then linking this up with the invisible nature of Yahweh should give us some insight. HIS creativity tells the story of a fallen creature that has rejected his salvation time after time throughout history.

Although these thoughts may be human intervention based on concoctions introduced by earlier stages of religious belief systems, one thing stands true; we live based on invisibility that we have never sought to understand but only to capitalize from. Jesus was sincerely preoccupied with this spirit that was in Him, and He refused to forsake Its invisibility while in the flesh, but at the same time, reasoning with those who were without an understanding of the light that existed within their humus bodies.

Once I met a person that told me a story about her girlfriend, who was terminally ill with cancer. The story took place in a hospital room. Present in the room with this bed-ridden friend was her father, her husband, and her friend, who had shared this story. While laying in the hospital half comatose, the young lady jumped up and asked, did you hear that? Her friend and family asked her, what is it that you heard? She replied, there it is again, but it's telling me that the room isn't clean, and I can't come until it's clean, so the father left the room; the young lady said again, the room still isn't clean, so her girlfriend left the room next, they heard crying in the room, and both the father and the friend returned to the room; she said again the room isn't clean in despair, so finally the husband left the room, and the young lady's spirit left her body immediately.

What was discovered was that the husband had been unfaithful for quite some time, nobody in the room knew this, but God had revealed this in the room. God knows us better than we know ourselves; God brings forward truths and only operates in truth and righteousness. God cleansed the room; this happens often, we're just not aware of these occurrences, we're blinded in this realm, but we have sight when we receive our kingdom vision. (LS)

In a book written by Andrew Murray, he explains Jesus's devotion to the created, the eternal connection with the humus being through the invisible spirit:

> *"This thought opens up to us further the reason why it is not the Spirit of God as such, but the Spirit of Jesus that*

could be sent to dwell in us. Sin had not only disturbed our relation to God's law, but to God Himself; with the Divine favour, we had lost the Divine life. Christ came not only to deliver man from the law and its curse but also to bring human nature itself again into the fellowship of the Divine life, to make us partakers of the Divine nature. He could do this, not by an exercise of Divine Power on man, but only in the path of a free, moral, and most real human development. In His own person, having become flesh, He had to sanctify the flesh and make it a meet and willing receptacle for the indwelling of the Spirit of God. Having done this, He had, in accordance with the law, that the lower form of life rose to a higher, only through decay and death, in death both to bear the curse of sin and to give Himself as the seed corn to bring forth fruit in us. From His nature, as it was glorified in the resurrection and ascension, His Spirit came forth as the Spirit of His human life, glorified into the union with the Divine, to make us partakers of all that He had personally wrought out and acquired, of Himself and His glorified life.

In virtue of His atonement, man now had a right and title to the fullness of the Divine Spirit, and to His indwelling, as never before. And in virtue of His having perfected in Himself a new holy human nature on our behalf, He could now communicate what previously had no existence -a life at once human and Divine. From henceforth, the Spirit, just as He was the personal Divine life, could also become the personal life of men. Even as the Spirit is the personal life principle in God Himself, so He can be it in the child of God: the Spirit of God's Son can now be the Spirit that cries in our heart, Abba, Father. Of this Spirit, it is most fully true, 'The Spirit was not yet, because Jesus was not yet glorified."

We, His people, are the surrounding context. God is communicating through the Spiritual that we are encapsulated with spiritual wisdom and that the Holy Spirit in us is explicitly breathed, but dirt covered, and He desires to have fellowship with that which is Holy. Now the danger of disregarding this literary instruction that is given to us by The Holy Spirit has been identified in the form of sin. How do we identify this surrounding context of sin? It comes by understanding the message that has been given to us, Basic Instructions Before Leaving Earth (Bible).

The Birth of Jesus was a paradigm shift in the world; this is what the New Testament represented. God had come back to reconcile the broken history through a divine-human body incarnated by His spirit. The prophetic message of the prophets in the OT had manifested itself! God desires that we seek His truths with an open mind; in this way, the Holy Spirit can reveal God's embodiment in Yeshua. Our expectations are set on the immediate miracles Jesus performed; even the disciples were energized by this. This same energy exists in believers today.

Although they seek spiritual truths, their hearts are far from God's message about the Kingdom of God here on earth. They desire the worldly religion in which Christ exists in their religion in the form of a theocracy. In this chaos, our minds can't receive the Holy Spirit's message about Yeshua's message concerning the Father's plan for salvation; this plan is to preserve us from the harm of a predisposed evil that desires to consume our minds, bodies, souls, and then send our remains into the grave and hold us there for eternity. This outcome is found in 1 Corinth. 10:13 and is solidified in Hebrews 4:12-13. God's plan for man is justified in Jesus, who is the incarnation of the "God Most High" whom we can't see, but should seek for a true foundational understanding of the sins we are faced with and how God has exhibited The Holy Spirit to come upon the flesh to bring forth, to teach and solidify the relationship with the invisible spirit that is manifested in creation through His people whom He has called into salvation to be delivered into His providence for eternal life. Our Minds must be opened to the Holy Spirit, who is the operative left through Yeshua's teachings to seek out those who call upon The Spirit of The Most High in truth and righteousness; in this way, we may pray using dialogue with questions we have about the kingdom of God.

    Once the Holy Spirit determines what we are looking for, we must trust the historical lessons. We shall study to show ourselves approved, our minds stay focused on the "Word" which is Yeshua's teachings in the Spirit of creation, and we will come into terms with Yahweh's plan for our salvation through the regenerative power of the invisibility of the Word that rests in us, which is the Invisible Nature of Yahweh.

We must remember that we stand in a position where truths exist in the form of wisdom, knowledge, and then research; we were not placed on the earth to die, nor to be taught death but how to transcend from the physical light body into the spiritual light realm. We are here on the earth to be taught survival skills in a rapidly advancing world that has hidden EL ELYON's truths about the migrations of clans that have settled throughout the planet that have developed menial survival skills in detriments void of truths. In this, ignorance has become their new norm based on manmade economies that have attracted the masses to form a global resistance against the most influential piece of information given to creation. This one piece of peace that has been eradicated from us is agape. Agape needs a partner. This partner is called love, and neither can exist without the humus temple given by Yahweh. Man needs love, love needs man, and love needs to be loved as well.

The question is, will we ever come into this realm of visible truths? Nothing will remain hidden, all truths will come to the surface, this is the plan for EL ELYON' infinite power over creation. The powers that be are those who hold authority and the power behind the throne refers to the people who exert influence without being formally in charge. Yahweh is the true colonial power; The Spirit is the KING of kings and LORD of lord's. The Invisible Nature of Yahweh rest rule and abide forever. Amen!

"If My people who are called by My name will humble themselves, and pray and seek My face, and turn from their wicked ways, then I will hear from heaven, and will forgive their sin and heal their land."

-2 Chronicles 7:14

REFERENCES

1. Kofahl, Robert E. "Awareness of God Series". The Parent Company Attributes of God/God is Spirit/Meaning/Conclusion March 13th 2018

2. Finney, Paul Corby The Invisible God: The Earliest Christians on Art [Preface viii 3rd paragraph] Copyright 1994 By Paul Corby Finney-First Published I 1994 by Oxford University Press, Inc. 198 Madison Avenue. New York, New York 10016 Date viewed

3. Deffinbaugh Robert L. The Invisibility of God [2nd Paragraph] (Genesis 32:22-30)

   (Exodus 24:9-11) (1Tim 1:17) (Dallas Theological Seminary) Published May 8th 2004.

4. "Celestial Hierarchy" Paranormity.com Celestial Hierarchy

5. "The Name Our Teachers Have Taught Us To Forget".

   Yahweh's Name." The House of Yahweh,.

6. Boucher, Jim. "Why Is God Invisible?". Therefore, God Exists

7. "The tabernacle was a very functional facility." https://bible.org/seriespage/32-tabernacle-dwelling-place-god-exodus-368-3943

8. Jud Davis. "The Creator Clearly Seen." Answers In Genesis,

9. Piper, John. "The Image Of God". Desiring God. March 1971

10. Malone, Andrew. "The Invisibility of God". A Survey of a Misunderstood Phenomenon

11. The Story of Christian Theology, 1999 by Olson Roger E. Inter Varsity Press. Page 58.

12. Scott, John. Quotes for topic: God-invisible. gracequotes.org

13. Ellicott Charles J. Commentary for English Readers "biblehub.com/commentaries/hebrews/1-3"

14. Rhett, Allain. 5Things Every Human Should Know About Light. Science 02.11.15

15. Got Question Ministries.

16. Stewart, Darius. The Darkness of Darkness. 2005-2007

17. DeAguiar Antonio "The Superior being known as God, Yahweh, The LORD" (Purple Caption)

18. Young Robert W. Page 3

19. Got Questions

20. Monroe, Dr. Miles "Prayer and Fasting in The Kingdom of God " (2014)

21. "2007 Yahweh's Assembly in Yahshua" [Yahweh's dwelling Place].

22. Mead, G.R.S. Mead (1900) Summary Of The Fragments Of The Book Of The Great Logos According To The Mystery

23. http://www.paranormality.com/celestial_hierarchy.shtml

24. What is the difference between Son of God and Son of Man?

25. Cine, Austin God is Transcendent and Immanent? How is that Possible?

26. Herrin, Joseph Yahweh, His Breath and His Word

27. Packer, JI. What does it mean that God is transcendent? https://www.gotquestions.org/God-transcendent.html

28. "Gil's Exposition of the Entire Bible." 2nd paragraph

29. Phillips, Gary W. Brown, William E. Stonestreet, John. "Making Sense of Your World" [Chapter 7. 186, 3rd paragraph] Sheffield Publishing Company 2008.

30. Murray, Andrew. The Spirit of Christ. Chapter 5. 4th paragraph

Please note that any direct quotes are written in their original form, which may contain grammar mistakes according to twenty-first century grammar rules.

About the Author

Dr. Tracey L. Milan was born in Evansville, Indiana. He comes from a family of eleven children, parented by Ira and Hazel Milan.

Dr. Milan has an undergraduate and Master's degree in Biblical history, and a Doctoral Degree in Theology. He currently resides in the Metro Atlanta, Georgia area with his wife and daughter.

Dr. Milan is a pragmatic, and solution oriented thinker, whose major influences are Dr. Myles Monroe and Dr. Ray Hagins, who shaped his critical thinking in studies and research relating to his Doctoral Theology degree.

"Throughout my life, I've listened and wondered what this life is really all about. In retrospect, I didn't realize this, but we the creatures, are positioned here on earth to carry the light placed within us. We are to break the curses of a broken kingdom and restore its true values. We transcend time as truth-bearers in a dirt body."

A WORD FROM DR. MILAN

I believe that the human condition is a fascinating journey; however, the syndrome that we are born into allows the humus creature the opportunity to adapt and evolve past the philosophical, political pragmatism, and religious theoretical dogmas presented. Throughout our lives we have been taught in error, survival skills that serve the elitist, their cultures, and their traditions.

Cages have been placed before us, we go in and out of these cages during our lifetime, but we must realize, we have the power to open and close the door to our cages, and most importantly, we are the proverbial lock and the key, so before you confine yourself to a cage know first that you have the authority to lock, and unlock your confinement. This key that consist of your internal wisdom given by Yahweh will unlock the power of the Kingdom and make it work in our lives.

Knowledge leads to understanding. Once we know the principles behind the keys, we can understand how they work in the Kingdom here on earth. This is exactly the problem with many believers today. We have "keys" that mimic "Scriptures" that most of us don't know how to use. We have an abundance of keys, but we don't know which key unlocks which lock pertaining to any particular scripture. It's like having all of this information from the Bible, but not knowing how to unlock its meanings. We have all of this power available to us but not knowing how to apply it. This is how we become prisoners in these cages, in and out of these cages in repetitious cycles due to a lack of knowledge.

Knowledge is power, and we must get our power back! The Word of God is important, but insufficient by itself for effective living as a believer. This is because most believers lack a proper Kingdom mindset. Life in the Kingdom is really about returning to the true laws that are the governing authority of God in the earth and learning how to live and function in that authority, you are the authority, so by knowing why and how you were placed in the visible Kingdom here on earth gives you the right to partake as a kingdom citizen. Part of understanding the Kingdom is learning how to use the keys (Authority) of the Kingdom.

The Kingdom of Heaven is God's desire and purpose for us. Yahweh' desire for us is to experience HIS true revelation for His creation on earth. God doesn't need us in heaven, HE brought heaven to the visible earth for us to witness HIS Kingdom to come: on earth as it is in Heaven! The Kingdom of heaven is not placed out of sight, it's the visible Kingdom that was placed in this planet. Yahweh placed the invisible Kingdom on a visible planet called earth; God colonized earth with the inherent qualities of heaven, but we must learn how to unlock its laws that have been bound by Satan. These keys have to be learned. A secret is anything that hasn't been shared, especially if somebody else is hiding information. Supernatural occurrences fall into this category, sometimes referred to as a miracle is something that humans cannot explain, an event or occurrence that seems to defy the laws of nature.

These men had seen Jesus walk on water, heal the sick, raise the dead, shrivel a tree by speaking to it, calm a storm, multiply bread, and many other "miraculous" things that were beyond the ken of human experience.

But to Jesus, none of these were miracles. He said, "These are no miracles; I'm just using keys. I know how to put them in the locks, and they are unlocking prosperity, unlocking healing, unlocking peace, and unlocking authority. Watch you and me will see the Kingdom at work, and also how it should work for you. My Father has given you the knowledge of the secrets of the Kingdom. I will teach you how to use the keys." Jesus left no doubt that the Kingdom was supposed to work for His ecclesia just as it worked for Him, for on the night before His death He told them.

"I tell you the truth; anyone who has faith in Me will do what I have been doing. He will do even greater things than these, because I am going to the Father.

And I will do whatever you ask in My name, so that the Son may bring glory to the Father.

You may ask Me for anything in My name, and I will do it."

-John 14:12-14

www.ingramcontent.com/pod-product-compliance
Lightning Source LLC
Chambersburg PA
CBHW030150100526
44592CB00009B/207